A Gift of Love

REFLECTIONS FOR THE TENDER HEART

CHARLES STANLEY

OLIVER NELSON™
THOMAS NELSON PUBLISHERS
Nashville

Published in Nashville, Tennessee, by Thomas Nelson, Inc.

ISBN 0-7852-6618-6

Printed in the United States of America

CONTENTS

For God so loved the world that He gave His only begotten Son, that whoever believes in Him should not perish but have everlasting life.

—JOHN 3:16

Introduction

A Gift of Love

The world is hurting for love. Ask any Christian counselor, pastor, or layperson who works with those who have suffered hurt, and they will tell you that love is a key issue. Lack of love—appropriate love—is the reason we have so much brokenness in our society.

You were created with a basic need for love. Amazing as it may sound, there is a love that can and will meet all of your needs. This love—God's love—is the only way to experience the love you so desperately desire and seek.

Many think they have to get their lives straightened out before they come to God, but that is not the way He operates. His love for you is unconditional. When He looks at your life, He sees only potential. No matter how dark your past has been or how bleak the present may seem, God's love can cleanse away the deepest sin: "For when we were still without strength, in due time Christ died for the ungodly. For scarcely for a righteous man will one die; yet perhaps for a good man someone would even dare to die. But God demonstrates His own love toward us, in that while we were still sinners, Christ died for us" (Rom. 5:6–8).

Jesus died so that you might have eternal life and love. What a tremendous gift He gives! And nothing this world has to offer can even come close.

Part 1

God— The Giver of Love

The Supreme Giver

The attributes of God are many—love, mercy, grace, forgiveness, kindness, and goodness. Yet none of these marvelous qualities would be known to mankind without the following character trait—giving.

God, by His own choice, holds nothing to Himself. He generously bestows His love, mercy, and grace upon man because He has sovereignly willed to share Himself and His bounty with us. We have life only because God has created us by an exercise of His will. We can receive salvation only because He wills to grant it.

The ultimate testimony to the Giver of all good things is, amazingly, the saints, the redeemed ones, "That in the ages to come He might show the exceeding riches of His grace in His kindness toward us in Christ Jesus" (Eph. 2:7).

The Supreme Giver's gift to men of salvation through Christ will resound throughout eternity. Believers will be the showcase, the tangible evidence, of His ever-giving heart. Thus, while we enjoy the eternal benefits of salvation, its fundamental root lies in the reality that our God is the preeminent Giver. All of the heavenly hosts will marvel at that truth without end.

Prayer: Father, thank You for being the Supreme Giver and giving the gift of love. That in the ages to come He might show the exceeding riches of His grace in His kindness toward us in Christ Jesus. (Eph. 2:7)

Because Your lovingkindness is better than life,
My lips shall praise You. (Ps. 63:3)

God demonstrates His own love toward us, in that while we were still sinners, Christ died for us. (Rom. 5:8)

THE INITIATOR OF LOVE

From the beginning of time, God has been the Initiator of love (1 John 4:10). In his book *Lectures in Systematic Theology*, Henry Thiessen writes, "He is unlike the gods of the heathen, who hate and are angry, and the god of the philosopher, who is cold and indifferent."

God loves us with a personal and intimate love. Those who have yet to discover the intimacy of God often view Him as being cool and demanding toward His creation. But nothing is farther from the truth. Even in the Old Testament, we find God constantly moving toward mankind in an effort to reveal more of Himself on an intimate basis.

Love motivates Him to do this. In fact, love is the motivating factor of every true relationship. It motivated the heart of God not to destroy man in the Garden of Eden, and it motivated Him to deliver Israel from the Egyptians.

Love brought down the walls of Jericho, and it was the motivation behind the coming of Christ. Love took our place on Calvary's cross and later rose from the grave. And love reaches out to us each day with freshness and hope.

You were created by love to live within its embrace. Many wonder how God could love them so deeply. But He does. He is Love, and He loves you and me.

Prayer: Lord, thank You for creating me by love to live within its embrace. I praise You for Your love that reaches out to me each day with hope.

Indeed it was for my own peace
That I had great bitterness;
But You have lovingly delivered
  my soul from the pit of corruption,
For You have cast all my sins behind Your back. (Isa. 38:17)

The LORD has appeared of old to me, saying:
"Yes, I have loved you with an everlasting love;
Therefore with lovingkindness I have drawn you." (Jer. 31:3)

"I have loved you," says the LORD. (Mal. 1:2)

Amazing Grace

It is little wonder that the hymn "Amazing Grace" is sung so resoundingly in churches across the world. Its vivid imagery reminds us of the preeminence of grace and its indispensable role in our salvation and sanctification—but what makes grace so amazing?

Grace is amazing because it is free. No currency exists that can ever purchase grace. We are usually suspicious of anything free, but God's offer comes without any hidden strings. He bore the cost for our sins (therefore, it is not cheap grace) so that He could extend it freely to any man on the basis of faith—not intellect, status, or prestige.

Grace is amazing because it is limitless. God's grace can never be exhausted. Regardless of the vileness or number of our sins, His grace is always sufficient. It can never be depleted; it can never be measured. He always gives His grace in fullness.

God's grace is amazing because it is always applicable. Do you need wisdom? God's grace provides it through His Word. Do you need strength or guidance? God's grace sustains you by His Spirit. Do you need security? God's grace supplies it through His sovereignty.

The amazing grace of God! Full and free! Without measure! Pertinent for your every need!

Prayer: O God, Your grace is amazing, full, and free. Thank You for grace without measure that is pertinent to my every need.

Being justified freely by His grace through the redemption that is in Christ Jesus. (Rom. 3:24)

And of His fullness we have all received, and grace for grace. (John 1:16)

So now, brethren, I commend you to God and to the word of His grace, which is able to build you up and give you an inheritance among all those who are sanctified. (Acts 20:32)

Three Pillars of Truth

You lose your job. Your spouse files for divorce. You discover that one of your children is on drugs. A loved one is diagnosed with cancer and given only six months to live. Such times are extremely disorienting. They strike with such intensity that your emotions can be buried beneath a tide of fear and anxiety.

Yet three pillars of truth can help you endure and triumph:

1. *God knows your problems.* Your woes have not taken God by surprise. He is aware of every detail of your troubles: "Your Father knows the things you have need of before you ask Him" (Matt. 6:8).

2. *God cares about your problems.* God loves you without limit. As the Good Shepherd, He will protect and defend you: "Do not be afraid nor dismayed because of this great multitude, for the battle is not yours, but God's" (2 Chron. 20:15).

3. *God is able to deal with your problems.* God has the power to handle your problems. Because He knows and cares, He will act according to His wisdom and will: "Humble yourselves under the mighty hand of God, that He may exalt you in due time, casting all your care upon Him, for He cares for you" (1 Peter 5:6–7).

Prayer: O Lord, thank You for the assurance that You know about my problems, You care about them, and You are able to deal with every issue.

Humble yourselves under the mighty hand of God, that He may exalt you in due time, casting all your care upon Him, for He cares for you. (1 Peter 5:6–7)

He said, "Listen, all you of Judah and you inhabitants of Jerusalem, and you, King Jehoshaphat! Thus says the LORD to you: 'Do not be afraid nor dismayed because of this great multitude, for the battle is not yours, but God's.'" (2 Chron. 20:15)

The Heart of God

Each year thousands of teenagers run away from home. Many never return. Can you imagine the grief and heartache of loving parents who long to reconcile with their children but are unable to overcome a son's or daughter's anger and rebellion?

Such is the heart of our loving God who diligently seeks to restore His relationship with sinful man: "When we were still without strength, in due time Christ died for the ungodly" (Rom. 5:6).

We are rebels—running away from the Lord Jesus Christ's offer of salvation and forgiveness, bent on pursuing our own goals and satisfaction apart from Him. Like immature children, we recoil from the Lord's holy presence:

> All we like sheep have gone astray;
> We have turned, every one, to his own way;
> And the LORD has laid on Him the iniquity of us all.
> (Isa. 53:6)

But God still waits. He refuses to withdraw His love, keeping His door of communion open at all times for the one who comes to faith in Christ: "When he was still a great way off, his father saw him and had compassion, and ran and fell on his neck and kissed him" (Luke 15:20).

The next move is yours. Will you receive His offer of peace

by personally receiving Jesus Christ as your Savior, Lord, and Life, or will you continue to run from His presence?

Prayer: Father, give me peace as I live in the shadow of Your presence today.

> When we were still without strength, in due time Christ died for the ungodly. (Rom. 5:6)

> All we like sheep have gone astray;
> We have turned, every one, to his own way;
> And the LORD has laid on Him the iniquity of us all.
> He was oppressed and He was afflicted,
> Yet He opened not His mouth;
> He was led as a lamb to the slaughter,
> And as a sheep before its shearers is silent,
> So He opened not His mouth. (Isa. 53:6–7)

Your Loving Father

Do you eagerly anticipate spending time alone with God, or are you fearful of His rebuke? Do you delight yourself in the Lord, or do you feel that Christianity is just another load to carry?

Christians should be the most joyful people on earth. The thrill of victory should dance on our tongues and souls since Christ has borne the agony of sin on His shoulders.

Perhaps the wonder of your relationship to Christ has been obscured by a misplaced emphasis on the character of God. Yes, He is holy; yes, He is a righteous Judge. But He always exercises these attributes within the framework of His mercy and grace.

When you were saved, God became your loving Father. You are His treasured, precious child. Nothing you do will change His steadfast, fatherly love. Run away if you will; rebel against His rule; yet the Father's heart does not turn away from you.

When you were saved, Christ became your faithful Friend. He is always there for you. You can never offend Him or disappoint Him since He knew you perfectly before you were saved and still He brought you to Himself. He wants to help you—regardless of the mess you may have made.

Prayer: O Lord, You love me despite my messes! Thank You for Your faithfulness!

Bless the LORD, O my soul;
And all that is within me, bless His holy name!
Bless the LORD, O my soul,
And forget not all His benefits:
Who forgives all your iniquities,
Who heals all your diseases,
Who redeems your life from destruction,
Who crowns you with lovingkindness and tender mercies.
(Ps. 103:1–4)

Love Revealed

"The highest proof of true friendship," writes Andrew Murray, "is the intimacy that holds nothing back and admits the friend to share our inmost secrets. It is a blessed thing to be Christ's servant; His redeemed ones delight to call themselves His slaves. Christ had often spoken of the disciples as His servants. In His great love our Lord now says, 'No longer do I call you servants, but, I have called you friends, for all things I heard from My Father I have made known unto you.'"

Since the beginning of time God has sought ways of revealing Himself to mankind—first in the Garden of Eden and later to the prophets. With the birth of His Son, God initiated an intimacy with man that can never be destroyed. Jesus' love for us was so great that He laid aside His royal robe in heaven and took up a towel and basin to serve those He came to save (John 13:1–17).

The next time you are tempted to think that God doesn't care if you hurt or if you are lonely, think about what it cost Him to come to earth. He did not come to judge or condemn; He came to demonstrate His personal love for you. Before He left heaven, He knew there would be a cross, and still He was willing to come to you.

When was the last time you told Him that you love Him?

Prayer: Lord, I just want to tell You that I love You. Thank You for being my Friend.

You call me Teacher and Lord, and you say well, for so I am. If I then, your Lord and Teacher, have washed your feet, you also ought to wash one another's feet. For I have given you an example, that you should do as I have done to you. (John 13:13–15)

Testing His Goodness

Knowing God is not simply an intellectual proposition. You know God in a manner much similar to the process of getting to know a human companion. J. I. Packer explains in his book *Knowing God*:

Knowing God is a matter of personal involvement—mind, will, and feeling. It would not, indeed, be a fully personal relationship otherwise. To get to know another person, you have to commit yourself to his company and interests and be ready to identify yourself with his concerns. Without this, your relationship with him can only be superficial and flavorless.

"Taste and see that the Lord is good," says the psalmist (Psalm 34:8). To "taste" is, as we say, to "try" a mouthful of something, with a view to appreciating its flavor. A dish may look good, and be well recommended by the cook, but we do not know its real quality till we have tasted it.

Similarly, we do not know another person's real quality till we have "tasted" the experience of friendship. Friends are, so to speak, communicating flavors to each other all the time, by sharing their attitudes both toward each other (think of people in love) and toward everything else that is of common concern.

The same applies to the Christian's knowledge of God, which, as we have seen, is itself a relationship between friends.

Prayer: I will bless You, Lord, at all times. Your praise will continually be in my mouth!

I will bless the LORD at all times;
His praise shall continually be in my mouth.
My soul shall make its boast in the LORD;
The humble shall hear of it and be glad.
Oh, magnify the LORD with me,
And let us exalt His name together. (Ps. 34:1–3)

Oh, taste and see that the LORD is good;
Blessed is the man who trusts in Him! (Ps. 34:8)

Our Greatest Lover

God is not afraid to love us, nor is He worried about our past failures. He is secure enough to love us unconditionally. Although He desires our love in return and longs for us to know His love in a personal way, He willingly leaves the decision up to us.

In loving us, He knows He is giving us something no one else can. The world will not offer unconditional acceptance as God does. Increasingly the standards of our society include progress, personality, and performance.

But unlike the world, God considers the most important things to be your heart and your acceptance of His Son as your Savior. Once you accept Him, love is set in motion in your life. From this vantage point, the Holy Spirit begins His work—molding, teaching, and guiding you in the ways of Christ.

Through His Spirit, you are given access to the greatest place of love—the presence of God. Here you find Him always available to listen to your hopes and frustrations. He knows your disappointments, and He is determined to bring good out of each heartache (Rom. 8:28).

God's love is a powerful protector, teaching you to avoid evil and to focus on His purpose for your life. He is your greatest Lover, the One who never gives up on you. His love never fails and in the end brings marvelous victory to all who are found in Him.

Prayer: Thank You for the protection of Your love, Lord, which teaches me to avoid evil and focus upon Your purposes for my life.

> We know that all things work together for good to those who love God, to those who are the called according to His purpose. For whom He foreknew, He also predestined to be conformed to the image of His Son, that He might be the firstborn among many brethren. (Rom. 8:28–29)

> As far as the east is from the west,
> So far has He removed our transgressions from us. (Ps. 103:12)

Putting God First

The church at Ephesus was commended for several positive qualities.

This hardworking body of believers was service oriented and put others first. When the believers saw a job to be done, they did it to the point of exhaustion. Even if the task was tough, they were steadfast, and they persevered until the need had been thoroughly met. In doctrine and theology, their knowledge and discernment were unexcelled.

What a portrait of a faithful church—almost. We read in Revelation 2:4: "I [God] have this against you, that you have left your first love." In the flurry of activity, this busy church had lost its former passion for the Lord.

You have met such people, those who are too caught up in the *what* to be concerned about the *why*. Maybe you are like this. You know that good works serve as a testimony of God's power in your life, but somehow when you stop moving so fast, you feel an unexplainable loneliness.

Remember that on God's scale, activity can never outweigh intimacy. Ask Him to remove from your life anything that takes priority over knowing Him. Tell God that you want your relationship with Him to take first place. He is faithful to renew your love.

Prayer: Dear God, I want my relationship with You to take first place. Renew my love for You right now.

To the angel of the church of Ephesus write, "These things says He who holds the seven stars in His right hand, who walks in the midst of the seven golden lampstands: I know your works, your labor, your patience, and that you cannot bear those who are evil. And you have tested those who say they are apostles and are not, and have found them liars; and you have persevered and have patience, and have labored for My name's sake and have not become weary. Nevertheless I have this against you, that you have left your first love." (Rev. 2:1–4)

Developing a Passion for God

The young convert shook his head in disbelief. He thought becoming a Christian would somehow inoculate him from future trouble. But Christianity does not provide immunity from heartache and trouble. However, in the heartache, God promises never to leave us. His protection and wisdom are available to all who are His.

Jesus said, "My sheep hear My voice, and I know them, and they follow Me. And I give them eternal life, and they shall never perish; neither shall anyone snatch them out of My hand" (John 10:27–28).

In 2 Corinthians 11, Paul provided an extensive list of the personal trials he faced as a result of his love for Christ. Several times he was beaten to the point of death. Many times he was rejected and ridiculed for his desire to further the kingdom of God.

What was the driving force behind his life? What kept Paul from giving up? A passion for God—the very thing that sustains us when fear and adversity threaten our existence.

A passion for God goes beyond simple fondness. It is a love for God that is constant, regardless of circumstances. A person with a passion for God is not likely to walk away from what God has given him to do. But if he should, he knows he can come home because God has a passion for him, and God's love never grows cold.

Prayer: Give me a passion for You, O Lord. Help me remain faithful to our relationship and what You have called me to do.

From the Jews five times I received forty stripes minus one. Three times I was beaten with rods; once I was stoned; three times I was shipwrecked; a night and a day I have been in the deep; in journeys often, in perils of waters, in perils of robbers, in perils of my own countrymen, in perils of the Gentiles, in perils in the city, in perils in the wilderness, in perils in the sea, in perils among false brethren; in weariness and toil, in sleeplessness often, in hunger and thirst, in fastings often, in cold and nakedness—besides the other things, what comes upon me daily: my deep concern for all the churches. (2 Cor. 11:24–28)

Rejecting the World

How do we measure our passion for God? We can't. Passion speaks of desire. It describes a heartfelt action we feel toward someone or something. God sees our hearts. He knows whether we have a passion for Him. There is no way to masquerade the sincerity of our passion.

Even after David sinned and caused God great heartache, the Lord called him a man after His own heart. How could that be? God looks beyond outward appearances to the very core of our being. He intimately knows us. In David's heart, God saw a true passion for Himself. Regardless of his failures, David loved God.

Yet God did not casually dismiss David's sin; his family bore the consequences of his behavior for generations. However, God's love toward David never changed. The promises God made to him as a young man remained intact. At the end of his life, David wrote,

> [God] has made with me an everlasting covenant,
> Ordered in all things and secure.
> For this is all my salvation and all my desire. (2 Sam. 23:5)

A passion for God comes when you reject the allure of the world and seek the praise of your loving and eternally devoted heavenly Father. He generously bestows grace and mercy to those who come to Him in humility.

Prayer: Heavenly Father, help me reject the allure of the world. Bestow Your grace and mercy on me as I face the circumstances of life today.

I will love You, O LORD, my strength.
The LORD is my rock and my fortress and my deliverer;
My God, my strength, in whom I will trust;
My shield and the horn of my salvation, my stronghold.
I will call upon the LORD, who is worthy to be praised;
So shall I be saved from my enemies. (Ps. 18:1–3)

Caring for His People

The Scriptures furnish several tender analogies of how God relates to His people.

God cares for us as a shepherd looks after his flock:

> Oh come, let us worship and bow down;
> Let us kneel before the LORD our Maker.
> For He is our God,
> And we are the people of His pasture,
> And the sheep of His hand. (Ps. 95:6–7)

Our God looks after His flock. He protects us, guides us, nourishes us. He comes quickly to our rescue when we are in need. He is the Good Shepherd whose eye is ever upon us and whose hand is ever ready to deliver and save.

God also cares for us as a father cares for his children:

> As a father pities his children,
> So the LORD pities those who fear Him. (Ps. 103:13)

God is our heavenly Father. Once saved, we are adopted into His family and share in the inheritance of blessings that come from His generous, benevolent hand.

The Bible stresses both the compassion and the discipline that are ours. God relates to us as children in need of direction, understanding, and correction. Let nothing dissuade you of God's yearning love for you.

Prayer: Thank You for Your love and compassion, Father. Thank You for Your discipline, which directs, corrects, and gives me understanding.

Oh come, let us worship and bow down;
Let us kneel before the LORD our Maker.
For He is our God,
And we are the people of His pasture,
And the sheep of His hand. (Ps. 95:6–7)

As a father pities his children,
So the LORD pities those who fear Him. (Ps. 103:13)

Taking the Initiative

Our God is an awesome God who has seized the initiative in revealing Himself to mankind. Apart from God's revelation, man would be mired in ceaseless ignorance and frustration.

John Stott paints this awe-inspiring portrait of God in his book *Basic Christianity*:

> "In the beginning God." The first four words of the Bible are more than an introduction to the creation story or to the book of Genesis. They supply the key which opens our understanding to the Bible as a whole. They tell us that the religion of the Bible is a religion of the initiative of God.
>
> Before man existed, God acted. Before man stirred himself to seek God, God has sought man. In the Bible we do not see man groping after God, we see God reaching after man.
>
> The Bible reveals a God who, long before it even occurs to man to turn to Him, while man is still lost in darkness and sunk in sin, takes the initiative, rises from His throne, lays aside His glory, and stoops to seek until He finds him.
>
> Before the foundation of the universe, God loved you and prepared a way for you to know Him. Meditate on that for a moment, and spill out your gratitude in worship.

Prayer: O Lord, thank You for preparing a way for me to know You before the foundation of the world. I praise You!

God, who at various times and in various ways spoke in time past to the fathers by the prophets, has in these last days spoken to us by His Son, whom He has appointed heir of all things, through whom also He made the worlds; who being the brightness of His glory and the express image of His person, and upholding all things by the word of His power, when He had by Himself purged our sins, sat down at the right hand of the Majesty on high, having become so much better than the angels, as He has by inheritance obtained a more excellent name than they. (Heb. 1:1–4)

Revealing Himself

God has taken the initiative in revealing Himself to mankind through several distinct means.

First, He has revealed Himself in creation. The heavens and earth and man himself are the handiwork of God. They testify to His goodness, His provision, His power. His creations are not products of chance and time but finely crafted masterpieces of His hand.

Second, God has revealed Himself through the Scriptures. Each verse in the sixty-six books of the Bible is God breathed, written by man through the inspiration of the Holy Spirit. The Bible tells us who God is, how we can know Him, and what His expectations are.

Third and preeminently, God has revealed Himself in the person and work of His Son, Jesus Christ. Jesus is God in the flesh. The invisible, infinite God became visible through Christ. In Christ was God's plan of salvation unveiled. In Christ, God reconciled the world to Himself so that all might be forgiven of sin and restored to the true knowledge of the living God.

Creation, the Scriptures, Jesus Christ—in each is the revelatory work of God displayed so that you might know and enjoy the precious gift of eternal life by faith in Christ.

Prayer: Dear heavenly Father, I thank You for the revelations of creation, Your Word, and Your Son, Jesus Christ.

The wrath of God is revealed from heaven against all ungodliness and unrighteousness of men, who suppress the truth in unrighteousness, because what may be known of God is manifest in them, for God has shown it to them. For since the creation of the world His invisible attributes are clearly seen, being understood by the things that are made, even His eternal power and Godhead, so that they are without excuse. (Rom. 1:18–20)

Rescuing the Lost

We ordinarily think of rescue operations occurring in distressful circumstances—a man trapped in a burning building, a child swept down a torrential stream, miners trapped and aching for breath in deep coal shafts. However, a man working in an office, a child fishing from the creek bank, or miners routinely extracting coal from black mining veins are not typical rescue scenarios.

It is difficult for many to view man in extreme need of rescue from God. We appear to be self-sufficient and able to muddle through even precarious situations. But that is not God's view. From His perspective—the right one—we are in desperate need of rescue. Our wealth, position, or status in our culture cannot deliver us. Our wisdom is barren, our technology useless.

Christianity is a rescue religion. It is the hand of God reaching down and pulling man out of his helpless state of sin. The Scriptures describe the unbeliever as dead in sin, a captive of the devil, living in spiritual darkness.

Such is the helpless state of mankind apart from God. But the God who cares will not leave us in this predicament if we will take His outstretched arm and be pulled to safety.

Prayer: O Lord, how I praise You that Your outstretched arm rescued me from sin and pulled me to the safety of Your loving embrace.

And you He made alive, who were dead in trespasses and sins, in which you once walked according to the course of this world, according to the prince of the power of the air, the spirit who now works in the sons of disobedience, among whom also we all once conducted ourselves in the lusts of our flesh, fulfilling the desires of the flesh and of the mind, and were by nature children of wrath, just as the others. (Eph. 2:1–3)

Expressing Your Love

Is your relationship with the heavenly Father one of duty or delight? God, who is Love, desires our fellowship with Him to be motivated by personal, growing, demonstrated love. God is a person. Although He could have existed without creating man, He made us for Himself. He wants such an intimate relationship with you that He sacrificed His Son for you, so you could be reconciled to Him forever.

As His child, you are free to love Him for all He is and for what He has done and will do for you. Each day is an opportunity to express your love for Jesus.

You can love Him by telling Him so. There is no such thing as true love in a marriage without verbal encouragement and praise. Likewise, God wants to hear the words of your lips that proclaim His excellence.

You can also tell Him you love Him by cheerful obedience. Work heartily at your task, knowing Christ is your Master. Carry out principles of Scripture He has laid on your heart. Serve others with compassion and understanding as Christ's ambassador on earth.

The more you know Christ, the more you love Him. The more you love Him, the more passionately you'll want to honor Him. It is a divine circle of love filled with blessings.

Prayer: I love You, Lord. I want to walk in obedience to You and fulfill Your plan for my life.

If you love Me, keep My commandments. (John 14:15)

He who has My commandments and keeps them, it is he who loves Me. And he who loves Me will be loved by My Father, and I will love him and manifest Myself to him. (John 14:21)

Jesus answered and said to him, "If anyone loves Me, he will keep My word; and My Father will love him, and We will come to him and make Our home with him." (John 14:23)

Renewing Relationships

Most Christians sincerely desire to love God and please Him—although if we are honest, there are seasons when we feel distant and detached from God.

Maybe you have become entrapped in the hectic pace of work, school, family, or other meaningful obligations. The times of communion with Christ have diminished. Perhaps you have been ensnared by a sinful habit that you will not abandon, and your guilt is so overwhelming, you are ashamed to approach Christ. Whatever the reason for your broken intimacy with God, there is good news. Jesus waits to embrace you now in the arms of unconditional, divine love.

The busy man and woman can stop today, take a deep breath, admit their misplaced priorities, and begin again to seek the kingdom of God. It may take time for feelings of intimacy to return, but fellowship can again be sweet.

If you have sinned, your guilt is washed away by the blood of the Cross. Confess your sin, receive His infinite forgiveness, and ask Christ to restore your soul. Once you are saved, no sin can keep you outside the love of God. He never condemns you.

God's mercies are new every morning. Great is His faithfulness. Return to Him, and the Spirit of God will rekindle your dimly burning wick.

Prayer: Father, please rekindle my dimly burning wick. Restore the intimacy of my fellowship with You.

Have mercy upon me, O God,
According to Your lovingkindness;
According to the multitude of Your tender mercies,
Blot out my transgressions.
Wash me thoroughly from my iniquity,
And cleanse me from my sin.
For I acknowledge my transgressions,
And my sin is always before me. (Ps. 51:1–3)

Divine Encounters

Many times in the psalms, David cried out to God to "restore," "revive," and "refresh" his soul. Sometimes he uttered his pleas out of a sense of desperation. Others came out of his desire to know God more intimately.

David was seeking a fresh encounter with God. You, too, often need times of renewed spiritual vitality when you can mount up on fresh wings of the soul. Although fresh encounters with God cannot be programmed or scheduled, they seldom happen apart from a lifestyle of meditation on God's Word combined with honest prayer.

God can break into your life explosively and suddenly or quietly and gradually. But when He does, you sense His presence and love anew. You are keenly aware of the Holy Spirit's active ministry within. You walk with a new assurance of God's help. Your problems may stay, your circumstances may remain, but you know God is in control. You are focused on His adequacy, not your inadequacy.

There is no end to the seasons of fresh encounters you may have with God. You can never exhaust His fullness. Personal encounters with God will help you see your own weaknesses and magnify the awesome reality of Christ's love for you. They are encounters of the closest kind that can refresh the driest soul.

Prayer: O Lord, restore me. Revive me. Refresh me. Give me a new, divine encounter with You.

> In the year that King Uzziah died, I saw the Lord sitting on a throne, high and lifted up, and the train of His robe filled the temple. Above it stood seraphim . . . And one cried to another and said:
>
> "Holy, holy, holy is the LORD of hosts;
> The whole earth is full of His glory!" . . .
>
> So I said:
>
> "Woe is me, for I am undone!
> Because I am a man of unclean lips,
> And I dwell in the midst of a people of unclean lips;
> For my eyes have seen the King,
> The LORD of hosts."
> (Isa. 6:1–3, 5)

Obstructing the Flow

Like a dammed river, God's love can be stifled, spilling over into an unproductive, uneventful Christian life, filled with knowledge but not wonder. God's love yearns to run its overflowing course, surging into the lives of others and ushering you fully into God's divine scheme. But you obstruct His benevolent flow of love through some common habits that keep your life bottled up in frustration and unfulfilled expectations.

A familiar spiritual logjam is self-centeredness: "Everything from God is for me." Yes, God's love is for your edification, but it is also for others. Your personal growth and blessing are only part of His overarching plan for the maturity of His body of believers.

Another commonplace impediment to the flow of God's love is anxiety. You worry and fret so much about your problems that God's love does not have a chance to branch out.

The only cure for such brooding is a confident trust in the sufficiency of God's love for your personal life. He loves you enough to care for your every need, freeing you to love others with renewed vitality and freshness.

Prayer: Dear Lord, please remove the obstructions that would hinder the flow of Your love through me.

Beloved, if God so loved us, we also ought to love one another. No one has seen God at any time. If we love one another, God abides in us, and His love has been perfected in us. By this we know that we abide in Him, and He in us, because He has given us of His Spirit. (1 John 4:11–13)

Worthy of Your Devotion

Some people have problems with the Lord Jesus Christ's command to love Him with all of their hearts, all of their souls, and all of their minds: "I do not like someone—even if that Someone is God—commanding me to love Him. I want my love to come freely."

Such a reservation melts when you consider why God sets the commandment of love above all others. As we allow the Holy Spirit to love Him through us, we love God with all of our strength because He is worthy of our devotion.

The Lord created the heavens and the earth and all that is in them, including you (Gen. 1:1; 2:7, 22). Christ has saved you from eternal destruction. He supplies all of your needs (Phil. 4:19). Christ Jesus died and rose again for you.

Understanding God's majesty and glory is the wellspring of your love. He has done so much for you. How can you not love such a One?

You also love God with all of your heart because He knows that devotion given to any other person or thing besides Himself is harmful. God created you for Himself. When your highest and noblest love is directed to something or someone else, you have been seduced into treachery. Loving God frees you from competing idols that only enslave you.

Prayer: Father, please free me from competing idols of this world that enslave me. Set me free to love and worship You.

Jesus said to him, "'You shall love the LORD your God with all your heart, with all your soul, and with all your mind.' This is the first and great commandment. And the second is like it: 'You shall love your neighbor as yourself.' On these two commandments hang all the Law and the Prophets." (Matt. 22:37–40)

Fostering Intimacy

What does it mean to be intimate with God? The believer who lives close to the Father's heart is free to express his feelings to Him. You do not have to be uptight with God. He knew every detail of your life the moment He created you. When you were saved, the Lord Jesus Christ understood all of your past failures and hang-ups and your future struggles.

Because you are now His child for all eternity, you can be completely honest with Him. You can pour out your hurts, your anger, your disappointments, your secrets, and your dreams to the Lord. He will never reject you (Heb. 13:5). You can never turn away His steadfast love.

There will be times when you do not understand what God is up to in your life. God's presence may seem distant. Because you have God's assurance of His presence, because of His unceasing activity on your behalf, and because of His love for you, you can still cling to Him. Refuse the advances of competing lovers—money, fame, power—and deny doubt and unbelief.

Have you the kind of intimacy with God that the Father is your most adored Friend? If not, confess your need for such a relationship and let Him gather you into His waiting arms.

Prayer: Heavenly Father, my heart cries out for an intimate relationship with You. Gather me into Your waiting arms. I want to be Your friend.

The LORD is near to all who call upon Him,
To all who call upon Him in truth. (Ps. 145:18)

He Himself has said, "I will never leave you nor forsake you." (Heb. 13:5)

You will seek Me and find Me, when you search for Me with all your heart. (Jer. 29:13)

Unconditional Love

We are prone to focus on the more malicious weapons in Satan's black armory—drugs, immorality, war, pornography, and crime. While these tools wreak havoc, there is a subtle tool that he uses to sabotage the Christian—guilt.

Through the ages, many believers have been rendered ineffective through feelings of guilt that hang over their hearts like a winter fog. A guilty Christian is most miserable.

Held long enough and deeply enough, guilt infects the emotions and weakens the will. Eventually growth halts, and a downward spiral escalates.

Do these characteristics describe your current experience? If so, please read on. If you are saved, all your sins have been forgiven—even your future ones. God has fully pardoned you from His judgment. You are unconditionally loved, regardless of your behavior. No one can condemn you any longer. Satan's attempts are illegal and fraudulent.

God forgives you; He loves you. Once and for all, reject Satan's false accusations, and experience God's love again. Simply open your heart and receive His love.

Prayer: Thank You for Your unconditional love, Lord. I open my heart and receive it right now!

The gift is not like that which came through the one who sinned. For the judgment which came from one offense resulted in condemnation, but the free gift which came from many offenses resulted in justification. For if by the one man's offense death reigned through the one, much more those who receive abundance of grace and of the gift of righteousness will reign in life through the One, Jesus Christ. Therefore, as through one man's offense judgment came to all men, resulting in condemnation, even so through one Man's righteous act the free gift came to all men, resulting in justification of life. (Rom. 5:16–18)

How God Sees You

There is a warped view in some evangelical circles that loving ourselves is selfish and wrong. Although Christians obviously are called to love God and others, loving ourselves in a biblical, nonnarcissistic fashion fosters a healthy spiritual balance.

We love ourselves properly when we see ourselves as God sees us. God declares His children to be His workmanship. He views us as men and women of inestimable worth—valuable enough to sacrifice His own Son on our behalf.

Your clothes, home, car, work, and friends do not determine your worth—God does. He values you so much that He desires to spend eternity with you.

We also love ourselves rightly when we treat ourselves properly. As God's masterpieces, we should take care of ourselves. Our bodies need balanced nutrition and exercise. Our personal grooming should be neat. We polish our furniture and wax our cars because they are objects of worth to us. Are we not worth more than they?

You are God's good and lovely creation. The more you affirm God's evaluation of yourself, the more you will adore Him and love others.

Prayer: Father, help me to see myself as You see me—a child of Your workmanship, a person of inestimable worth.

Let them praise the name of the LORD,
For He commanded and they were created. (Ps. 148:5)

I have made the earth,
And created man on it.
I—My hands—stretched out the heavens,
And all their host I have commanded. (Isa. 45:12)

We are His workmanship, created in Christ Jesus for good works, which God prepared beforehand that we should walk in them. (Eph. 2:10)

God's Gift of Grace

The grace of God is meant for heavy-duty, regular use in your daily routines. Your ability to enjoy and experience its power and provision in the mundane hinges upon your loving obedience to God's Word and His Spirit. In his book *My Utmost for His Highest,* Oswald Chambers explains the divine coupling of grace and obedience:

> No man is born either naturally or supernaturally with character; he has to make character. Nor are we born with habits; we have to form habits on the basis of the new life God has put into us.
>
> We are not meant to be illuminated versions but the common stuff of ordinary life exhibiting the marvel of the grace of God.
>
> . . . The tiniest detail in which I obey has all the omnipotent power of the grace of God behind it. If I do my duty, not for duty's sake but because I believe God is engineering my circumstances, then at the very point of my obedience the whole superb grace of God is mine through the atonement.

Grace is for washing dishes when you are tired; playing with the children when you would rather be watching the ball game; inviting a lonely neighbor over for dinner when you would rather be alone. It works in the daily grind when you are willing to obey.

Prayer: Lord, thank You for Your gift of grace, which empowers me for the details of life.

God is able to make all grace abound toward you, that you, always having all sufficiency in all things, may have an abundance for every good work. (2 Cor. 9:8)

Therefore, whether you eat or drink, or whatever you do, do all to the glory of God. (1 Cor. 10:31)

By the grace of God I am what I am, and His grace toward me was not in vain; but I labored more abundantly than they all, yet not I, but the grace of God which was with me. (1 Cor. 15:10)

Part II

Jesus Christ—The Gift of Love

The Sum of God's Purpose

An esteemed theologian was once asked the greatest truth of the Bible. He quickly replied: "Jesus loves me, this I know, for the Bible tells me so."

When Jesus was asked what was the greatest commandment of all, He distilled the sum of God's purpose into love: loving God with all the heart, mind, and soul and loving our neighbor as ourselves (Matt. 22:37–39).

Love is God's prime mover. It is not some kind of vague, impersonal emotion but personal affection for the crown of His creation: you and me. God is love. We are saved because God "so loved the world" that He willingly and unilaterally sacrificed His Son for our sake (John 3:16). He took the initiative. We can give love only because "He first loved us" (1 John 4:19).

Because of His spectacular love expressed through Jesus Christ, we can daily abide under the constant umbrella of His loving care as children of God, enjoying all the benefits of His lavish love—His presence, protection, comfort, help, guidance, strength, and peace.

Jesus loves you. He died for you. If you believe in Him, you are kept forever in His loving embrace.

Prayer: Jesus, thank You for taking the initiative and loving me first. I love You!

We love Him because He first loved us. (1 John 4:19)

If we receive the witness of men, the witness of God is greater; for this is the witness of God which He has testified of His Son. He who believes in the Son of God has the witness in himself; he who does not believe God has made Him a liar, because he has not believed the testimony that God has given of His Son. (1 John 5:9–10)

Eternal Friendship

Jesus Christ is man's best Friend. Christians are not only forgiven of our sins and gifted with eternal life; our relationship with God is transformed from enmity to intimacy. Abraham was called a "friend of God" (James 2:23). Jesus' disciples were not merely students but "friends" (John 15:13). During His earthly ministry, His disposition toward even the most despised men—tax gatherers—was characterized by friendliness.

As your Friend, Jesus loves you as no other can. He loves you when you behave miserably. When others reject you and misunderstand you, Jesus embraces you, comforts you, and counsels you. As your holy Friend, Jesus listens with compassion. You can complain, argue, gripe, moan, cry, or grieve. He sympathizes with every emotion without turning you away.

Jesus' friendship is unceasing. There is never a moment when you are without His intimate presence. At the heights of loneliness, Jesus is with you, in you, longing for you to look to Him for His unfailing help and consolation.

Is Jesus your Friend? Do you see Him only in a stern light, or do you hear Him call: "Friend, come and spend time with Me today"?

Friendship with God is life's greatest pleasure and eternity's everlasting reward. It is a gift of love.

Prayer: Lord, thank You for Your eternal friendship. It is my greatest pleasure. I appreciate Your gift of love.

You are My friends if you do whatever I command you. No longer do I call you servants, for a servant does not know what his master is doing; but I have called you friends, for all things that I heard from My Father I have made known to you. You did not choose Me, but I chose you and appointed you that you should go and bear fruit, and that your fruit should remain, that whatever you ask the Father in My name He may give you. (John 15:14–16)

Accepting God's Gift

After becoming Christians, many people feel that if only they had known the truth about God's love, they would have accepted Jesus as their Savior years earlier. The fact is, many of us might have accepted Christ earlier had we known the depth and length of God's love and forgiveness. But we didn't. Satan had blinded our eyes to the truth.

Salvation is a free gift of God. It is a work of grace and not of human achievement. Jesus Christ paid the once-and-for-all sacrificial price for your sin at Calvary. Nothing you do can ever do what Jesus did for you at Calvary.

God's love is eternal and available for every area of your life. People who reject His love and forgiveness usually establish conditional rules and regulations with hopes of becoming more acceptable to God.

However, it is not a matter of becoming more acceptable. When we came to Christ for salvation, He made His unconditional love and acceptance known to us.

Have you trusted Jesus as your personal Savior, or are you striving to achieve a higher level of goodness before you make a commitment? Only Jesus is worthy of that position, and yet He freely offers us a chance to draw near to God and receive the gift of eternal life.

Prayer: Thank You for the free gift of salvation, Father. Thank You for Your eternal love that is available for every area of my life.

For God did not send His Son into the world to condemn the world, but that the world through Him might be saved. He who believes in Him is not condemned; but he who does not believe is condemned already, because he has not believed in the name of the only begotten Son of God. And this is the condemnation, that the light has come into the world, and men loved darkness rather than light, because their deeds were evil. (John 3:17–19)

Embracing Christ's Friendship

The book of Hosea is a compelling love story of God's unfailing, steadfast care for His people despite their unfaithfulness, ingratitude, and repeated rebellion. Foreseeing their eventual restoration, Jehovah God makes this endearing statement to a stiff-necked people:

> "And it shall be, in that day,"
> Says the LORD,
> "That you will call Me 'My Husband,'
> And no longer call Me 'My Master.'" (Hos. 2:16)

This expresses the deepest desire of God's heart for us—that we would know Him intimately as a wife knows her mate.

Jesus expresses the same sense of endearment when He tells His disciples and us that we are not simply His servants but His friends with whom He desires to fellowship on the deepest, most compassionate level.

If you view God as your heavenly Father who longs to embrace you, sustain you, and lift you up on wings of divine love, your walk of faith can soar. Jesus is your close, concerned Friend as well as your Master. You can weep with Him, grieve with Him, laugh with Him, even complain to Him. His love for you will never fail, never wane, never subside.

Prayer: How I praise You for Your love that never fails! Thank You for weeping with me, grieving with me, laughing with me, and listening to my complaints!

"And it shall be, in that day,"
Says the LORD,
"That you will call Me 'My Husband,'
And no longer call Me 'My Master.'" (Hos. 2:16)

I will betroth you to Me forever;
Yes, I will betroth you to Me
In righteousness and justice,
In lovingkindness and mercy;
I will betroth you to Me in faithfulness,
And you shall know the LORD. (Hos. 2:19–20)

Seeking the Lost

The Pharisees were appalled that Jesus associated with sinners. They publicly grumbled about Jesus' actions to show their disgust for what they called loose, disreputable behavior. Sometimes He even ate meals with the sinners and social outcasts!

Jesus responded immediately. He wanted them to understand that His real mission is to save lost mankind—all who recognize that they are separated from God by their sin and believe that He pays the price for them. Jesus wanted the Pharisees and scribes to know how much each lost soul means to Him, how much He is willing to do to restore the person to fellowship with God.

Jesus, the true Shepherd, compared His love for sinners to a shepherd boy searching for one lost sheep. This shepherd boy left his other ninety-nine sheep safe in the fold to seek the missing one. The shepherd was personally responsible for each sheep in his care. If something happened to one of them, he had to give an account to the owner of the flock. Imagine this boy's relief and joy when he finally carried the wandering one home.

Jesus has this same love for you. He wants you to know your infinite value, to come to Him and rest in His care.

Prayer: Jesus, thank You for being my Shepherd—for seeking me, loving me, and leading me.

He spoke this parable to them, saying: "What man of you, having a hundred sheep, if he loses one of them, does not leave the ninety-nine in the wilderness, and go after the one which is lost until he finds it? And when he has found it, he lays it on his shoulders, rejoicing." (Luke 15:3–5)

Focusing on Christ

In Colossians 1:28 Paul wrote, "Him we preach." We are to tell others about Jesus. But how can we effectively do this if our hearts are divided and we lack a true passion for God?

Our world is filled with various passions—a passion for sports, food, personal achievement, money, recognition—the list could go on. Many people reason that God is not interested in what they do outside church. But Jesus had a different answer: "'You shall love the LORD your God with all your heart' . . . is the first and greatest commandment" (Matt. 22:37–38).

He told His disciples: "To obey is better than sacrifice." The Jews took great pride in offering sacrifices. They believed it was sufficient in uprighting their lopsided relationship with God. However, they offered the sacrifices out of a desire to be noticed by others.

Do you have a true passion for God? Is He your first thought in the morning, your constant companion throughout the day, and your last thought at night? Do you consider what He wants for your life above your personal desires?

You may achieve good things, but you will never fully experience Christ until your focus and passion are for Him and Him alone.

Prayer: O Lord, let my focus and passion be for You and You alone!

To them God willed to make known what are the riches of the glory of this mystery among the Gentiles: which is Christ in you, the hope of glory. Him we preach, warning every man and teaching every man in all wisdom, that we may present every man perfect in Christ Jesus. To this end I also labor, striving according to His working which works in me mightily. (Col. 1:27–29)

Moving Beyond Legalities

The lawyer thought he had the perfect question, the inquiry that would blow an unrecoverable hole in the defense and win the case.

He looked at his fellow prosecutors, glanced at the eager spectators, then stepped forward boldly to demand an answer: "Teacher, which is the great commandment in the Law?"

You can almost hear the hush that fell over the crowd. What would Jesus say? If Jesus selected just one of their many laws, He would devalue the rest of the commandments. If He refused to answer, He would be discredited as a valid teacher and scriptural authority.

But Jesus swept all categories and former definitions aside when He said, "'You shall love the LORD your God with all your heart, with all your soul, with all your mind, and with all your strength.' This is the first commandment." Once again, Jesus was moving them beyond the technicalities to the ultimate truth: nothing and no one else is more important than loving the Lord with the totality of your being.

Every biblical directive points to a relationship with Jesus Christ forever. When He is your all-consuming passion, you safely sidestep all legalistic traps.

Prayer: Become my all-consuming passion, Lord. Let me love You with all my heart, soul, mind, and strength.

Then one of the scribes came, and having heard them reasoning together, perceiving that He had answered them well, asked Him, "Which is the first commandment of all?" Jesus answered him, "The first of all the commandments is: 'Hear, O Israel, the LORD our God, the LORD is one. And you shall love the LORD your God with all your heart, with all your soul, with all your mind, and with all your strength.' This is the first commandment. And the second, like it, is this: 'You shall love your neighbor as yourself.' There is no other commandment greater than these." (Mark 12:28–31)

An Example of God's Love

Stumbling to the bathroom, he began his usual routine of getting ready for work. As he reached for the shaver to remove the night's stubble from his face, he noticed his son coming through the doorway.

Yawning and rubbing the sleep out of his eyes, he climbed up on the clothes hamper beside his father and began going through the same motions, only on an imaginary basis.

Curious about the whole event, the dad continued by following up with a stiff splash of aftershave. In uninterrupted motion, his son reached for the same bottle, poured a small amount of lotion in the palm of his hand, and planted two firm pats on his face.

He then looked up at his father and said, "I'm getting ready for work just like you, Dad." Then the father realized the importance of his life's example. One day his son would grow to be just like him in many ways.

Jesus came to earth to save mankind from sin. But the implications of His incarnation go much farther. He came as an example of God's love toward us. We are His children created by Him to walk in the likeness of His Son, just as Jesus was a reflection of the image of God. We are called to reflect His love and grace to others.

Prayer: Father, thank You for the divine example of Your love demonstrated through Your Son. Let me reflect His image to people today.

Jesus said to him, "Thomas, because you have seen Me, you have believed. Blessed are those who have not seen and yet have believed." And truly Jesus did many other signs in the presence of His disciples, which are not written in this book; but these are written that you may believe that Jesus is the Christ, the Son of God, and that believing you may have life in His name. (John 20:29–31)

UNDERSTANDING THE FATHER

God sent His Son, Jesus Christ, to earth to reestablish the personal line of communication that was severed by the Fall. Salvation is the first step we take toward knowing the intimate side of God's love.

Jesus came so we might understand the Father's undivided devotion toward us. Through His unconditional acceptance and grace, we find healing for our broken lives and hope for the future.

But some say, "If only you knew my past, you would know why Jesus would never love me." To thoughts like these, Jesus replies, "Come to Me, all you who labor and are heavy laden [that is, burdened by sin, anxious thoughts, and feelings of fear], and I will give you rest. Take My yoke upon you and learn from Me, for I am gentle and lowly in heart, and you will find rest for your souls. For My yoke is easy and My burden is light" (Matt. 11:28–30).

Christ's birth provided the freedom man longed to experience. Through His life and death, our past is made clean (Isa. 1:18). Through His resurrection, we find strength and courage to try again. He is your intimate Friend, One who is never ashamed to gather you in His strong arms of love.

Prayer: Thank You for freedom, Lord! Thank You for erasing the mistakes and sins of my past.

Come to Me, all you who labor and are heavy laden, and I will give you rest. Take My yoke upon you and learn from Me, for I am gentle and lowly in heart, and you will find rest for your souls. For My yoke is easy and My burden is light. (Matt. 11:28–30)

Blessed Because He Came

The New International Version translates Hebrews 11:1 this way: "Faith is being sure of what we hope for and certain of what we do not see." From this point Scripture details many examples of godly faith—that is, things men hoped for but did not receive until their faith had been severely tested.

In some cases, they never saw the answers to their prayers, but that did not stop them from believing God. Some scholars call the time between Malachi and the birth of Christ "the silent years." The fact is, Israel waited four hundred years to hear God's voice once again. Can you imagine what it would be like not to hear from God for hundreds of years? All that men and women such as Simeon and Anna had to go on was pure faith that God would do exactly what He said He would do (Luke 2:21–38).

How blessed we are that Jesus came! The prophets longed for His coming, but God chose us to be the ones to receive the gift of His presence. No longer is His life mere words recorded on sheets of papyrus. Instead, He is a living, breathing reality.

Have you accepted God's eternal gift of hope by placing your trust in the unchanging, unshifting reality of Jesus Christ? His birth is an anchor to the soul and a promise fulfilled that you can firmly trust.

Prayer: I place my trust in You, O Lord. You are the anchor of my soul.

Behold, there was a man in Jerusalem whose name was Simeon, and this man was just and devout, waiting for the Consolation of Israel, and the Holy Spirit was upon him. And it had been revealed to him by the Holy Spirit that he would not see death before he had seen the Lord's Christ. So he came by the Spirit into the temple. And when the parents brought in the Child Jesus, to do for Him according to the custom of the law, he took Him up in his arms and blessed God and said:

"Lord, now You are letting Your servant depart in peace,
According to Your word;
For my eyes have seen Your salvation." (Luke 2:25–30)

Setting the Example

Part of the disciples' training was practical application. Jesus would teach; then He would bring the lesson to life through a parable or a real-life experience. By walking on water, He displayed supernatural abilities. Withdrawing to be alone with the Father, He portrayed His devotion and set an example for His disciples to do likewise.

A group of people gathered, numbering more than four thousand; they were hungry, and Jesus willingly fed them. It was His way of saying, "I am the bread of life" (John 6:48). Peter, overwhelmed by all he had witnessed, made the following confession: "You are the Christ, the Son of the living God" (Matt. 16:16).

Jesus came to point men to God. He also came to identify personally with each one of us. The people prayed that Jesus was the One who would set Israel free from years of Roman oppression. They didn't understand His greatest desire was to restore the love that man had lost for God.

What is your greatest desire? Is it to know God's love and affection? During the Transfiguration, Peter was so overcome with emotion that he could only whisper his heart's desire: "Rabbi, it is good for us to be here; and let us make three tabernacles" (Mark 9:5).

Jesus was much more than flesh and bone; He was God, and Peter wanted to be found hidden in His love.

Prayer: Lord, my greatest desire is for You. Hide me in Your love.

That Christ may dwell in your hearts through faith; that you, being rooted and grounded in love, may be able to comprehend with all the saints what is the width and length and depth and height—to know the love of Christ which passes knowledge; that you may be filled with all the fullness of God. (Eph. 3:17–19)

Lessons of Love

The lessons of love are difficult. Peter and the disciples found this to be true. On a rocky hillside they listened as Jesus spoke words that seemed to them alien and far removed from what they were accustomed to hearing. What the group did not understand was that these words signaled a change in the direction of the Lord's earthly ministry.

Up to that point Jesus concentrated on healing the sick and speaking words that brought harmony and peace to the hearts of those who drew near to hear Him. But His time on earth was coming to a close. It was time for the cold, hard facts of love to be revealed. The cross stood before Him, and the only way men and women are saved is to face it as well. Christ was commissioned for a purpose. God's plan included a final sacrifice, and no sentimental ploy of Satan could interrupt it.

Finding the truth too hard to hear, many abandoned Jesus. Those who had truly tasted the depths of God's love knew they could never return to their former way of life.

Love that is cushiony and doesn't require responsibility is not true love. When trials come your way, stand firm in the love God has given you through His Son. If you will trust Him, you will find that His love, tested and tried at Calvary, is eternally strong no matter what the challenge.

Prayer: Heavenly Father, help me to learn the difficult lessons of love. I praise You that Your love, tested at Calvary, is eternally strong despite the challenges I face.

> From that time Jesus began to show to His disciples that He must go to Jerusalem, and suffer many things from the elders and chief priests and scribes, and be killed, and be raised the third day. Then Peter took Him aside and began to rebuke Him, saying, "Far be it from You, Lord; this shall not happen to You!" But He turned and said to Peter, "Get behind Me, Satan! You are an offense to Me, for you are not mindful of the things of God, but the things of men." (Matt. 16:21–23)

FAITHFULNESS IN HARD TIMES

When Jesus explained how He had to go to Jerusalem where He would suffer and die, His disciples were filled with anguish and fear. Peter immediately tried to rebuke the Lord by saying, "Far be it from You, Lord; this shall not happen to You!" (Matt. 16:22). But Jesus stood firm. Like the others, Peter could not yet see the strength of eternal love supporting and protecting the Son of man.

Perhaps you are going through a difficult season, and you don't understand why God has allowed you to suffer. Be assured that God loves you and that He has a plan for your life. Even when darkness seems to surround you, God is at work. His love never stops, never gives up, and never gives in to devastating circumstances.

Jesus understood how painful it would be for His disciples to hear of His impending death. He ministered comfort when it was needed and eternal hope when the emotional darkness became too much for them to bear, and He will do the same for you.

Prayer: Dear Lord, keep me faithful during the hard times. Thank You for Your love that never stops, never gives up, and never gives in to negative circumstances.

> Jesus said to His disciples, "If anyone desires to come after Me, let him deny himself, and take up his cross, and follow Me. For

whoever desires to save his life will lose it, but whoever loses his life for My sake will find it. For what profit is it to a man if he gains the whole world, and loses his own soul? Or what will a man give in exchange for his soul?" (Matt. 16:24–26)

Hope in Desperate Times

Paul wrote, "According to my earnest expectation and hope that in nothing I shall be ashamed, but with all boldness, as always, so now also Christ will be magnified in my body, whether by life or by death" (Phil. 1:20).

Upon entering a city, Paul immediately went into the local temple, synagogue, or meeting place to present the gospel message to the Jews. However, his words were often met with anger and rejection. But God did not allow Paul to suffer disgrace.

He had given the Jewish people a promise: He would send the Messiah to them for their redemption. Over the years their hearts had hardened. In piety they worshiped God but refused His offer of redemption. Going through the motions of worship cannot save anyone.

Israel missed God's greatest gift of love when they rejected the Lord Jesus Christ. The years they spent in suffering were meant to draw them closer to God. Yet even that bitter fate did not move them to heartfelt worship.

When you live above the hardness of your circumstances as Paul did, God will protect and keep you. He will also preserve the message of hope He has commanded you to take to a lost and dying world. Don't let others' criticism keep you from obeying God. When you feel discouraged, go to Him. Ask Him to plant Scripture in your heart, so you may experience His hope and love in desperate times.

Prayer: Lord, plant Your Word in my heart, use me for Your kingdom purposes, and let me experience Your hope and love in desperate times.

> I know that this will turn out for my deliverance through your prayer and the supply of the Spirit of Jesus Christ, according to my earnest expectation and hope that in nothing I shall be ashamed, but with all boldness, as always, so now also Christ will be magnified in my body, whether by life or by death. For to me, to live is Christ, and to die is gain. (Phil. 1:19–21)

ANSWERING THE CALL

Not many people liked Zacchaeus very much. He was not the best-looking man in Jericho; he was so short, he could not see over the heads of the people crowded around him when Jesus came to town.

Yet that was not the reason the people of Jericho disliked him. Zacchaeus was a tax collector, an employee of the Romans responsible for gathering the taxes from the Jews. Not only that, but he was in a position of authority over other tax collectors.

When he heard Jesus was coming, he was as excited as the rest of the city. He lost no time scampering up a sycamore tree to get a clear view when the Man everyone yearned to see passed that way.

We don't know all the emotions in Zacchaeus's heart or what circumstances God had been using in his life to prepare him for this moment. But we do see a picture of Jesus' love and acceptance: "Zacchaeus, make haste and come down, for today I must stay at your house" (Luke 19:5).

He moved even faster coming down from the tree than he did climbing up: "So he made haste and came down, and received Him joyfully" (Luke 19:6). Why? He responded to Jesus' overflowing, unconditional love.

This is the same love that Jesus offers you—no questions, no qualifications. All you have to do is to answer His call.

Prayer: Thank You, Jesus, for being the Lover of my soul, a Friend who will not let me down.

> Now behold, there was a man named Zacchaeus who was a chief tax collector, and he was rich. And he sought to see who Jesus was, but could not because of the crowd, for he was of short stature. So he ran ahead and climbed up into a sycamore tree to see Him, for He was going to pass that way. And when Jesus came to the place, He looked up and saw him, and said to him, "Zacchaeus, make haste and come down, for today I must stay at your house." (Luke 19:2–5)

Looking for Love?

In a sad country song that was popular several years ago, the singer recalled his past romances. "Lookin' for love in all the wrong places" was how he summed up his failure to find love that truly satisfied his heart and need for acceptance.

The Samaritan woman certainly knew how it felt to miss out on love. She had been married five times and was living with a man who wasn't her husband when she met Jesus. The woman had faced five rejections—how bruised and scarred her emotions must have been. She went to the well at the hottest part of the day just to avoid the scorn and disapproval of her neighbors.

Jesus' words cut straight to her hurts and deepest desires: "Whoever drinks of the water that I shall give him will never thirst. But the water that I shall give him will become in him a fountain of water springing up into everlasting life" (John 4:14).

Have you tried to find complete fulfillment in human relationships? Jesus' love is eternal, unchanging, sustaining; all other affections are temporary and someday will prove disappointing. You can trust in the Savior, who will not let you down or leave you comfortless. Jesus is the Person to go to when you are looking for true love.

Prayer: O Lord, I have come to the right source. Fill me—baptize me—with Your love.

Jesus answered and said to her, "Whoever drinks of this water will thirst again, but whoever drinks of the water that I shall give him will never thirst. But the water that I shall give him will become in him a fountain of water springing up into everlasting life." The woman said to Him, "Sir, give me this water, that I may not thirst, nor come here to draw." (John 4:13–15)

SHARING THE GOOD NEWS

If you have ever had a best friend, you know what it feels like not to be able to get enough time with him. When you thoroughly enjoy someone's company, it is no trouble at all to arrange ways to spend time with that person. Going a season of time without seeing your friend can be a real emotional letdown.

The same is true of your relationship with the Lord. Jesus is your most intimate Friend, the One who loves you with agape love. If you go a period of time without fellowshipping with Him, you will experience the effects of separation from your very lifeline—an inner sadness and loneliness that can be satisfied only by drawing near to Him again (James 4:8).

The more time you spend with the Lord and in meditation on His truth, the greater your passion to know Him. The Samaritan woman at the well discovered this principle in the short amount of time she spent talking with Jesus.

When Jesus offered her living water, her curiosity was piqued. She was flooded with many emotions, including surprise and wonder. The woman was so excited about this new relationship that she left her water pot and ran to tell others in town (John 4:28–42).

That is what happens when you know the Lord; your excitement grows and, with it, your fervor for sharing His good news with others.

Prayer: Father, give me a fervor for sharing the good news of Your gift of love.

Draw near to God and He will draw near to you. (James 4:8)

But what things were gain to me, these I have counted loss for Christ. Yet indeed I also count all things loss for the excellence of the knowledge of Christ Jesus my Lord, for whom I have suffered the loss of all things, and count them as rubbish, that I may gain Christ . . . that I may know Him and the power of His resurrection, and the fellowship of His sufferings, being conformed to His death. (Phil. 3:7–8, 10)

An Eternal Symbol

Even though intimacy with God involves a journey that takes place over a lifetime, the Bible teaches that there is never a time when God is unaware of you. He knows all about you—all the good and all the bad—and His love for you remains infinitely the same.

Salvation is just the beginning of a much closer relationship that builds and deepens over time. God is already there waiting for you to love and respond to Him. The more you grow in your knowledge of Him, the more you will come to understand that God gave everything He had to offer when He gave His Son to you as an atonement for your sins.

The cross where Jesus died is an eternal symbol of His personal care and love toward you. But the work of the Cross does not end at Calvary. It continues in every aspect of life, calling you to leave your old ways—your sin—behind and follow Him with an intimate, loving desire.

Only through intimacy can He teach you to view life with hope and compassion. This is especially needed today when there is so much discouragement. Never be discouraged. Jesus Christ is your strength and your sure hope. He overcame the jeers and insults of man so that He might prove His love to you.

Prayer: O Lord, You have searched me and known me. I am so glad You are acquainted with all of my ways.

O LORD, You have searched me and known me.
You know my sitting down and my rising up;
You understand my thought afar off.
You comprehend my path and my lying down,
And are acquainted with all my ways. (Ps. 139:1–3)

Your Security

"Pastor," the woman began, "I just don't understand why people treat me the way they do."

"What do you mean? Do you feel mistreated?" he asked gently.

"Not exactly. It seems that many of my friends and even my family don't appreciate all that I do for them. It seems the harder I work to please them, the less they thank me for it. They take me for granted! Don't I count for something?"

"Yes, you do," the pastor replied, "but not for the reasons you think." The woman leaned forward and listened intently. "You don't have to work for their acceptance and approval, but you are choosing to do so. Do you know why?"

"Because if I don't, they won't like me," she said with a determined voice.

"Well, if they don't like you because of something you have or haven't done, your relationship has the wrong basis anyway. But the real reason you don't have to work for their approval is that your personal worth is already established in Christ."

"What does that mean?"

"It means that Jesus loves and accepts you unconditionally. You can live in absolute security, giving to others freely without worrying about what you get in return. Others will sense your unselfish motivation, and the nature of your relationships will change in time."

Prayer: Father, thank You for the absolute security of my relationship with You. Let this be reflected in my relationship with others.

I thank my God always concerning you for the grace of God which was given to you by Christ Jesus, that you were enriched in everything by Him in all utterance and all knowledge, even as the testimony of Christ was confirmed in you, so that you come short in no gift, eagerly waiting for the revelation of our Lord Jesus Christ, who will also confirm you to the end, that you may be blameless in the day of our Lord Jesus Christ. (1 Cor. 1:4–8)

The Greatest Sacrifice

Some people find it hard to believe that God is involved in the physical elements of the world today. They regard Him as being removed and distant from His creation. But this is far from the nature of God. He would never speak life into the universe only to abandon it.

His sole intent is to reveal His love for you. And while He desires your love in return, He is committed to not pressuring you into a relationship with Him. For love to be sincere, it must come from the heart.

Jesus told His disciples that the greatest commandment a man or woman could fulfill was to love the Lord God above everything else (Matt. 22:37). Just as God came to earth to seek a personal relationship with us, we must seek His love above everything else.

Doing this requires personal sacrifice. However, God sacrificed His love first for us by sending His Son to earth to die for our sins on Calvary's cross. He could have remained in heaven where He was worshiped and adored, but He came to us so that we would know that He is a God who cares.

You can know without a shadow of doubt that God loves you. Ask Him to reveal His personal love for you. No matter what you are facing, God is still committed to you through the power of His eternal love. When you call to Him with a heart of love, He always answers.

Prayer: Lord, I really do love You. Reveal Your personal love to me today in a new way.

Come and see the works of God;
He is awesome in His doing toward the sons of men.
He turned the sea into dry land;
They went through the river on foot.
There we will rejoice in Him.
He rules by His power forever;
His eyes observe the nations. (Ps. 66:5–7)

A Radical Display

The nation of Israel grieved God's heart continually by chasing after other gods and withholding their devotion and adoration from Him. To provide this errant nation with a living illustration of His righteous grief and anger, God gave the prophet Hosea an unusual command. He told him to wed a harlot and begin a family with her.

Without questioning, Hosea obeyed and took the prostitute Gomer to be his wife. Though she wandered and continued in an unfaithful lifestyle, Hosea obeyed the Lord and did not cast her away. The book of Hosea contains God's words to the people of Israel as revealed through Hosea's dramatic example of steadfast love.

The moving poetry of this book also reveals the longing of God for uninterrupted intimacy with His people. Can you feel the agony of separation in these words?

> How can I give you up, Ephraim?
> How can I hand you over, Israel? . . .
> My heart churns within Me;
> My sympathy is stirred.
> I will not execute the fierceness of My anger. (Hos. 11:8–9)

God longs for the same intimate relationship with you. He would do anything to get your love—and He did. In the most radical display of all time, He provided His Son, Jesus Christ, as the means to make such fellowship possible. God is the passionate and faithful Lover of your soul.

Prayer: Father, thank You for the radical display of Your love—Jesus Christ. I praise You for being the passionate and faithful Lover of my soul!

> My people are bent on backsliding from Me.
> Though they call to the Most High,
> None at all exalt Him. (Hos. 11:7)

> Through the LORD'S mercies we are not consumed,
> Because His compassions fail not.
> They are new every morning;
> Great is Your faithfulness. (Lam. 3:22–23)

WHAT A FRIEND!

Do you remember having a best friend as a child? This person went everywhere with you, from recess in the schoolyard to adventures around the neighborhood. You had small fights and squabbles occasionally, but you stuck by each other when a difficulty came along.

As an adult, you may have a friend like this today, but you are certainly aware that such friends are rare indeed. The blessing of a friend who understands your deepest thoughts and needs and loves you through the hard times is a gift from the Lord. It is important to recognize, however, that the best friend in the whole world can still let you down at times. It is not a cliché to state that Jesus is your only true Friend.

Joseph Scriven, an Irishman born in 1819, discovered this truth in a powerful way. The night before he was to be married, his beloved fiancée drowned. Grieving deeply, Scriven decided to move to Canada and begin a new life, dedicated entirely to letting the Lord use him in others' lives. Out of this experience and several others, he penned the words to the favorite hymn, "What a Friend We Have in Jesus."

Can you imagine writing this poetry after going through such pain? Scriven saw the Lord's faithfulness. He knew firsthand that when all earthly supports and emotional props disappear, Jesus is there to love and comfort eternally.

Prayer: Thank You for Your unfailing love and comfort, Jesus. Thank You for Your being there for me in difficult times.

I waited patiently for the LORD;
And He inclined to me,
And heard my cry.
He also brought me up out of a horrible pit,
Out of the miry clay,
And set my feet upon a rock,
And established my steps.
He has put a new song in my mouth—
Praise to our God;
Many will see it and fear,
And will trust in the LORD. (Ps. 40:1–3)

God with Us

One of the most debilitating emotions is loneliness. Maybe you've felt that way in a hospital or emergency room, in a new city or job, or even in the midst of friends and family. Feeling as if there is no one to care or share with is a terrifying sensation. It can even be deadly.

That is why one of the most comforting names given to our Savior is Immanuel—God with us. Because of the indwelling Christ, believers are never separated from His permanent presence. We are in Christ and He is in us. What an encouragement! What a comfort! What an assurance! We always have a shoulder to lean on—the broad shoulders of Immanuel. We always have Someone to listen to our heartache—our constant Companion and Friend, Jesus.

The gods of other religions are usually in some far-off, remote corner, stoically seated in a seat of perfection. Not so with our Creator and Redeemer. Once He is in us, He will never leave us, abandon us, or forget us.

Don't let the adversary and accuser rob you of the peace and joy that come from experiencing and enjoying the sweet presence of our God. No sin, no deed, no trial can ever diminish the full presence and acceptance of Christ once you have become His child through faith.

God is with you. God is for you. God loves you. Allow His presence to fill any void.

Prayer: You are with me. You are for me. You love me. Lord, fill any void in my life with Your divine presence.

> Then Paul stood in the midst of the Areopagus and said, "Men of Athens, I perceive that in all things you are very religious; for as I was passing through and considering the objects of your worship, I even found an altar with this inscription: TO THE UNKNOWN GOD. Therefore, the One whom you worship without knowing, Him I proclaim to you: God, who made the world and everything in it, since He is Lord of heaven and earth, does not dwell in temples made with hands." (Acts 17:22–24)

A Divine Scapegoat

Through repeated usage, the term "scapegoat" has become quite familiar to our secular culture. Its meaning—an innocent party being blamed—has its roots, however, in an ancient Hebrew ritual known as the Day of Atonement.

This holy day took place once each year. The high priest took two male goats as a sin offering for the iniquities of the people. One goat was slaughtered, and its blood was sprinkled on the mercy seat. The remaining goat was sent into the wilderness after the high priest had placed his hands on the goat's head and confessed the sins of the nation over it. Through this "scapegoat" observance, God showed His mercy to the Israelites, allowing Him to continue His covenant relationship with them.

In much the same way, Jesus became the divine Scapegoat for the sins of the world. He was and is "the Lamb of God who takes away the sin of the world!" (John 1:29). Our sins were placed on Him at Calvary. Indeed, our sins put Him there. Jesus took the blame so that we could live.

Have you trusted in His atonement? Have you come to Him for the forgiveness of your sins? Have you been healed of your transgressions through His sacrifice?

Prayer: Lord, thank You for healing me of transgressions. Thank You for being the scapegoat for my sins.

The next day John saw Jesus coming toward him, and said, "Behold! The Lamb of God who takes away the sin of the world!" (John 1:29)

And looking at Jesus as He walked, he said, "Behold the Lamb of God!" (John 1:36)

Who Himself bore our sins in His own body on the tree, that we, having died to sins, might live for righteousness—by whose stripes you were healed. (1 Peter 2:24)

HE IS OUR PEACE

Europe trembled. Hitler's menacing armies were poised for a strike against Czechoslovakia. Attempting to appease the dreaded dictator, England's Prime Minister Neville Chamberlain traveled to Germany and, on September 29, 1938, signed the infamous Munich Pact. Upon his return, Chamberlain triumphantly announced, "I believe it is peace for our time." A year later Germany invaded Poland and World War II began.

Was Jesus' talk of peace like Chamberlain's optimistic boast? After all, why talk of such when war, violence, greed, and ill will still abound? Although Jesus talked much about peace and promised the disciples (and us) that He would leave us His peace, He did not ignore the reality of the world's conflict.

That's why His Passover message concerning peace was immediately followed by this clarification: "In the world you will have tribulation" (John 16:33). Jesus was a realist. There is nothing of evasiveness or idealism in His ministry. How, then, could He promise peace: "These things I have spoken to you, that in Me you may have peace" (John 16:33)?

Christ Himself is our peace. His presence, strength, and comfort are ours in every gale, for He is always with us.

Prayer: You are my peace, Lord. I claim Your presence, strength, and comfort today!

These things I have spoken to you, that in Me you may have peace. In the world you will have tribulation; but be of good cheer, I have overcome the world. (John 16:33)

Peace I leave with you, My peace I give to you; not as the world gives do I give to you. Let not your heart be troubled, neither let it be afraid. (John 14:27)

May the Lord of peace Himself give you peace always in every way. (2 Thess. 3:16)

Christ, Our Life

NBA superstar Larry Bird was sidelined for an entire regular season following foot surgery. Commenting on his inactivity, Bird admitted that he was having a difficult time making the adjustment: "Basketball is my life. I don't know what to do if I'm not playing."

What did Bird mean by that statement? What he must have been expressing was that basketball—the games, the practices, the plays, the excitement, the players—consumed his time and attention.

When Paul wrote about "Christ who is our life" (Col. 3:4), he was making reference to the fact that the Christian should be centered and concentrated on the person of Christ. "Christ, our life" means that the believer is regularly engaged in the disciplines of prayer, Bible study, meditation, and obedience.

Regardless of our circumstances, we are to seek Christ and His will above all else. Our minds are tuned to His wisdom, our hearts to His presence, and our hands to His purpose.

Wherever we go and whatever we do, "we are ambassadors for Christ" (2 Cor. 5:20) as reflected in our actions and our attitudes. When we live preeminently for Christ and His kingdom as we make our daily rounds, then "Christ is our life."

Prayer: Be my life, O Lord. Then make me an ambassador of life to others.

When Christ who is our life appears, then you also will appear with Him in glory. (Col. 3:4)

He died for all, that those who live should live no longer for themselves, but for Him who died for them and rose again. (2 Cor. 5:15)

Now then, we are ambassadors for Christ, as though God were pleading through us: we implore you on Christ's behalf, be reconciled to God. (2 Cor. 5:20)

Lord of All

The increase in the number of new small businesses represents one of the fastest growing segments of our economy. Typically such businesses are initiated by men and women who grew weary of the corporate maze. "I was tired of having my life run by someone else. I wanted to be my own boss" is their consensus.

This sense of self-determination can negatively influence other aspects of our existence when taken to its extreme. We want to direct and determine our current and future destiny with as little interference as possible. The notion of another individual having a greater stake in our lives than ourselves is shocking and even offensive. Yet Jesus Christ makes that startling claim to all of mankind. He alone has the title and guarantee to our lives.

He is Lord of all—over the living and the dead—whether or not they recognize Him as Lord. Christian and pagan alike will one day confess His total ownership of all (Rom. 14:11). He is Lord of all men by creation. The heavens and the earth and all they contain (including you and me) are His. He is Lord of believers by redemption, having purchased the souls of men through His shed blood.

Your destiny is not in your hands; it lies in the hands of Jesus Christ, Lord of all, who loves you and gave Himself for you.

Prayer: Dear heavenly Father, I am so thankful that my destiny is not in my hands. It is in Your hands—the One who loved me so much that You gave Yourself for me.

For if we live, we live to the Lord; and if we die, we die to the Lord. Therefore, whether we live or die, we are the Lord's. (Rom. 14:8)

For it is written:
"As I live, says the LORD,
Every knee shall bow to Me,
And every tongue shall confess to God." (Rom. 14:11)

He has on His robe and on His thigh a name written: KING OF KINGS AND LORD OF LORDS. (Rev. 19:16)

HE IS LORD

Knowing Christ as Lord has very practical implications. It means that you owe your allegiance to Him. The things of earth—money, prestige, authority, possessions—compete for that allegiance. But you belong to Christ alone, not the company store.

It means that His agenda, not yours, dictates your life. You can dream and have ambitions, but you must always be willing to submit them to "what is that good and acceptable and perfect will of God" (Rom. 12:2). Christ must have the right to navigate your existence according to His wisdom and plan.

It means that you must always see yourself as a servant. Christ, who is Lord, became the servant of all. Your relationship to Him and to others is, thus, one of willing servitude, manifesting the heart of the Chief Servant.

It means that you are accountable to Christ for your actions and words. You are not free to do what you want but only what He wants. Christ, your Lord, is also your Judge. You must answer to Him. He will overlook nothing.

When Christ is not just Lord but your Lord, your work, family, habits, and affections become everyday workshops that display the Master's handiwork.

Prayer: Father, let my work, family, habits, and affections be workshops to display Your handiwork.

I beseech you therefore, brethren, by the mercies of God, that you present your bodies a living sacrifice, holy, acceptable to God, which is your reasonable service. And do not be conformed to this world, but be transformed by the renewing of your mind, that you may prove what is that good and acceptable and perfect will of God. (Rom. 12:1–2)

And He sat down, called the twelve, and said to them, "If anyone desires to be first, he shall be last of all and servant of all." (Mark 9:35)

You Have It All

Every individual who has trusted Jesus for his salvation has received the Source for his most compelling needs in the person of the indwelling Christ.

Christ is the Bread of Life. He is the Sustenance who nourishes our innermost being. Our hunger for meaning and purpose in life is fully satisfied in Christ. He is meaning; He is purpose. We want not for significance in life when we have Christ as our life.

Christ is the Water of Life. He channels His all-sufficient life through our earthen vessels, drenching us with His joy, peace, love, hope, contentment, strength, and steadfastness. He quenches our thirst for self-worth, assuring us of our inestimable value to Him. He freely gives us His abundant life.

Christ is the Light of Life. He enlightens us with eternal truth, bequeathing us wisdom for the journey. He sheds His light upon what is truly valuable so that we can pursue the things that are profitable, not foolishly chasing empty dreams or false, deceiving philosophies.

When you have Christ, you have it all—meaning, purpose, life in its fullest sense, truth, and wisdom. You belong to the Creator, Sustainer, and End of all things.

Prayer: Father, You are my Creator, Sustainer, and End of all things. I have it all in You!

Jesus said to them, "I am the bread of life. He who comes to Me shall never hunger, and he who believes in Me shall never thirst. But I said to you that you have seen Me and yet do not believe. All that the Father gives Me will come to Me, and the one who comes to Me I will by no means cast out." (John 6:35–37)

Bearing Fruit

Concerning John 14:9, Oswald Chambers writes:

These words were not spoken as a rebuke, nor even with surprise; Jesus was encouraging Philip to draw closer. Yet the last person we get intimate with is Jesus. Before Pentecost the disciples knew Jesus as the One who gave them power to conquer demons and to bring about a revival (Luke 10:18–20). It was a wonderful intimacy, but there was a much closer intimacy to come . . . "I have called you friends . . ." (John 15:15).

True friendship is rare on earth. It means embracing someone in thought, heart, and spirit. The whole experience of life is designed to enable us to enter into this closest relationship with Jesus Christ. We receive His blessings and know His Word, but do we really know Him?

It is a joy to Jesus when a disciple takes time to walk more intimately with Him. The bearing of fruit is always shown in Scripture to be the visible result of an intimate relationship with Jesus Christ (John 15:1–4).

Once we get intimate with Jesus we are never lonely and we never lack for understanding or compassion. We can continually pour out our hearts to Him without being perceived as overly emotional or pitiful. The Christian who is truly intimate with Jesus will never draw attention to himself but will only show the evidence of a life where Jesus is completely in control.

Prayer: Take control, Lord. Let my life demonstrate evidence of Your presence.

> I am the true vine, and My Father is the vinedresser. Every branch in Me that does not bear fruit He takes away; and every branch that bears fruit He prunes, that it may bear more fruit. You are already clean because of the word which I have spoken to you. Abide in Me, and I in you. As the branch cannot bear fruit of itself, unless it abides in the vine, neither can you, unless you abide in Me. (John 15:1–4)

Part III

The World—The Recipient of Love

SEEKING THE LORD

She couldn't explain how the relationship got out of hand. One day they were only friends; a week later they had crossed a line of intimacy that could not be taken back. In tears, she asked God to forgive her.

Slowly a passage of Scripture came to mind: "I beseech you therefore, brethren, by the mercies of God, that you present your bodies a living sacrifice, holy, acceptable to God, which is your reasonable service. And do not be conformed to the world, but be transformed by the renewing of your mind" (Rom. 12:1–2).

At first, she frowned at the obvious rebuke and wondered how God could continue loving her. But then she sensed His grace at work in her life. The words that were sent to convict were also words of direction. God's desire for her was not for her to give up and be bound by feelings of failure, but for her to give herself afresh and new to Him. In seeking His forgiveness, she found restoration and hope.

God's loving desire for you is that you would come to know Him as Lord over every area of your life. As His child, you have immediate access to His throne. Your life is a trophy of His grace, and nothing you do can keep you from Him when you seek Him with all your heart.

Prayer: Dear Lord, transform me by Your Word. I offer my body as a living sacrifice to You.

[God] desires all men to be saved and to come to the knowledge of the truth. For there is one God and one Mediator between God and men, the Man Christ Jesus, who gave Himself a ransom for all, to be testified in due time. (1 Tim. 2:4–6)

Spending Time with God

She bustled out of bed the moment the alarm went off and dressed. Swallowing a piece of toast on her way to work, she hopped in the car and flipped on the radio. The office was fast-paced as usual, so she hardly had time to think about anything but the boss's projects. She was so tired when she got home that she made a quick dinner and flopped down on the sofa for a little TV before turning out the lights. One thing was missing from her day—silence. Peace and quiet. She hadn't set aside any time to commune with the Lord and discover new, exciting truths about her Savior.

God won't compete with anyone or anything else for your attention. To experience His fellowship in the fullest sense, you must approach Him with an undistracted heart. He knows your anxieties, problems, and hectic schedule even better than you do.

Consciously set aside all other interests and concerns to read your Bible and pray. Make other quiet times during the day as well, hushed moments when the Lord has a chance to impress His words on your mind and fill you with a special sense of His presence.

When you do, you see Him as He is, and you can join with all of heaven declaring, "Holy, holy, holy is the Lord of hosts."

Prayer: Dear God, help me order my priorities to spend quality time with You. Let me see You as You really are.

The four living creatures, each having six wings, were full of eyes around and within. And they do not rest day or night, saying:

"Holy, holy, holy,
Lord God Almighty,
Who was and is and is to come!" (Rev. 4:8)

The twenty-four elders fall down before Him who sits on the throne and worship Him who lives forever and ever, and cast their crowns before the throne, saying:

"You are worthy, O Lord,
To receive glory and honor and power;
For You created all things,
And by Your will they exist and were created."
(Rev. 4:10–11)

A Wholehearted Seeker

In the annals of the kings of Israel and Judah, King Josiah was a bright light in a world of darkness.

Why? Because at the age of sixteen, he had one driving motivation in life—to seek the Lord. Most of the rulers before him had erected altars to idols and promoted the worship of false gods among the people. His own father was so despicable that his servants killed him. But Josiah persevered in his pursuit of fellowship with God and cleansed Judah of all traces of idolatry by burning the evil altars and desecrating their holy places. So zealous was he in his love for the Lord that he ground the objects of false worship to powder.

Josiah learned a valuable lesson from his forefathers: when you don't actively pursue your relationship with God, you drift into sin. Believing that Jesus is your Lord and Savior gives you an eternal relationship with Him, but it does not guarantee intimate fellowship. Fellowship is an abiding closeness you seek through prayer and study of God's Word. Oneness doesn't come automatically, without interest or effort. You build intimacy with Him as you yearn for His truth and look for it with determination and purpose.

Are you a wholehearted seeker?

Prayer: Make me a wholehearted seeker, Lord. I don't want to drift into sin.

Josiah was eight years old when he became king, and he reigned thirty-one years in Jerusalem. And he did what was right in the sight of the LORD, and walked in the ways of his father David; he did not turn aside to the right hand or to the left. For in the eighth year of his reign, while he was still young, he began to seek the God of his father David; and in the twelfth year he began to purge Judah and Jerusalem of the high places, the wooden images, the carved images, and the molded images. (2 Chron. 34:1–3)

Checking Your Vital Signs

When you go to the doctor for a physical, he first checks your vital signs. Blood pressure, pulse, respiration rate, temperature—they all give a general picture of your health. Any problems in these major areas signal the doctor to probe further to determine what needs additional treatment.

To see how you are growing in your desire for intimacy with the Lord, you can look at certain spiritual vital signs. With the Bible as a guide, assess yourself in these areas to see how you are moving toward closer fellowship with Him.

Your faith is strengthening. The big problems of yesterday don't seem insurmountable anymore.

You have emotional and intellectual confidence in His provision. Psalm 42:1 is a constant prayer of your heart: "As the deer pants for the water brooks, so pants my soul for You, O God."

Your thirst to know Him causes you to seek His truth continually. Your focus is on His care and not on potential consequences. Adversities and trials become opportunities for rejoicing and praise instead of self-pity and worry. In His power you see past the temporary hurt to the promised victory.

Ask God to use the results of this checkup to move you closer to Him. As you seek Him every day, you'll come to love Him more.

Prayer: Strengthen my faith, Lord. Give me confidence in Your provision and an ever-increasing thirst for Your truth.

> Now by this we know that we know Him, if we keep His commandments. He who says, "I know Him," and does not keep His commandments, is a liar, and the truth is not in him. But whoever keeps His word, truly the love of God is perfected in him. By this we know that we are in Him. He who says he abides in Him ought himself also to walk just as He walked. (1 John 2:3–6)

Keeping God's Commandments

"If you really love me, you won't just say it; you'll show it," a father says to his little girl. More than anything, he wants to see love in action. Words aren't enough. When his daughter does what he says, especially without being reminded, he knows that she cares, that she wants to please him.

The connection between love and obedience is inseparable. Jesus is very clear about what pleases Him: "If you love Me, you will keep My commandments." Nothing else substitutes for genuine submission to God's will. Not even the noblest good work is of any value when it doesn't comply with God's established standards revealed in His Word.

King Saul learned this lesson the hard way when he performed a sacrifice that God did not authorize. The prophet Samuel reproached him, saying:

> Has the LORD as great delight in burnt
> offerings and sacrifices,
> As in obeying the voice of the LORD?
> Behold, to obey is better than sacrifice,
> And to heed than the fat of rams. (1 Sam. 15:22)

When Jesus is your Savior, you have a growing hunger to please Him, to live a holy life, and to express your gratitude by doing what He says. Ask Him to show you His truth. He will satisfy your heart as you seek His ways.

Prayer: Lord, I want to please You in every area of my life. Reveal to me Your truth. Let me walk in obedience in Your ways.

Samuel said:
"Has the LORD as great delight in burnt offerings and sacrifices,
As in obeying the voice of the LORD?
Behold, to obey is better than sacrifice,
And to heed than the fat of rams.
For rebellion is as the sin of witchcraft,
And stubbornness is as iniquity and idolatry."
(1 Sam. 15:22–23)

But the mercy of the LORD is from everlasting to everlasting
On those who fear Him,
And His righteousness to children's children,
To such as keep His covenant,
And to those who remember His commandments to do them.
(Ps. 103:17–18)

Longing to Know Him

The word *passion* often carries with it sensual or negative connotations. We think of crimes of passion or an immoral act committed in the heat of passion.

Passion is a powerful emotion, an overwhelming love or desire that supersedes all other interests. It does not have to be negative; in fact, Jesus tells us, "Love the Lord your God with all your heart, and with all your soul, and with all your mind." That is what it means to love God passionately.

R. C. Sproul describes it this way in his book *One Holy Passion*:

> If we are to progress in godliness we need to fan the flames of a holy passion. We need a single-minded desire to know God. We follow Jesus who went before us.
>
> He was moved by a single passion—to do the will of His Father. His meat and drink were to do His Father's will . . . Jesus revealed the Father to us and called us to imitate His own pursuit. His priority is set before us—to seek first the Kingdom of God and His righteousness.

Do you have passionate feelings for God? Is a love relationship with your Lord and Savior the all-consuming drive of your existence? He wants it to be. Ask Him today to give you a longing to know Him more.

Prayer: O God, let me be consumed with a passion to know You better! Order my priorities to seek Your kingdom and righteousness above all else.

> O God, my heart is steadfast;
> I will sing and give praise, even with my glory.
> Awake, lute and harp!
> I will awaken the dawn.
> I will praise You, O LORD, among the peoples,
> And I will sing praises to You among the nations.
> (Ps. 108:1–3)

Expressing Appreciation

A despicable man lived in a graveyard and cut his flesh with rocks. Every time people tried to tie him up, he burst his bonds and ran back to the tombs or to the desert, wherever the demons drove him (Luke 8:29).

No wonder he was overcome with gratitude when Jesus set him free from demonic dominion. The healed man fell down and begged his newfound Savior to let him come along. Nothing else mattered to him; Jesus had restored him, and he understood that now his life belonged to Him, in wholeness and completion. He knew the horror of the existence from which Jesus had saved him, so he was thrilled all the more for a chance to start over.

When you recognize the sin and hopelessness from which Jesus has pulled you by His matchless grace, you have the same deep, abiding appreciation. The apostle John said, "In this is love, not that we loved God, but that He loved us and sent His Son to be the propitiation for our sins" (1 John 4:10).

You love your Savior because He loved you first and He gives you a new life that you cannot get for yourself. Do you have a passion to tell others what He has done for you? You cannot be silent when you feel the fullness of His love.

Prayer: Thank You, Lord, for loving me and sending Your Son to be the propitiation for my sins.

Then they went out to see what had happened, and came to Jesus, and found the man from whom the demons had departed, sitting at the feet of Jesus, clothed and in his right mind. And they were afraid. They also who had seen it told them by what means he who had been demon-possessed was healed . . . So it was, when Jesus returned, that the multitude welcomed Him, for they were all waiting for Him. (Luke 8:35–36, 40)

SUBMITTING TO GOD

A woman sought to obey Christ on a deeper and more personal level. The Lord impressed 1 John 2:15 on her heart. Total obedience to Christ was being hindered by a personal possession she treasured.

Though it was quite painful, she obeyed what she knew the Lord had told her. She sold her treasure to a woman who was a non-Christian. The woman's obedience had a profound effect on the life of the nonbeliever who was aware of the inner struggle. They became friends, and in time the nonbeliever accepted Christ as her Savior.

Today, that new believer is working in Christian ministry. She even returned the item she had purchased to her friend, at the Holy Spirit's prompting. One woman's simple obedience brought someone into God's kingdom.

A burning love for Christ means submission to God's instruction. Your love for Him is demonstrated by your obedience. The joy this holds for you is the great blessing He gives in return.

Are you willing to lay yourself and all you own before the Lord? Is Christ at the center of your life, or are you holding on to something else that may be hindering your devotion? Your answer will help you determine the true measure of your love.

Prayer: Dear heavenly Father, I submit to You. I lay down my life before You. Please become the center of my life.

Do not love the world or the things in the world. If anyone loves the world, the love of the Father is not in him. For all that is in the world—the lust of the flesh, the lust of the eyes, and the pride of life—is not of the Father but is of the world. And the world is passing away, and the lust of it; but he who does the will of God abides forever. (1 John 2:15–17)

Good Works

Good works are as much a part of a believer's life as faith. Everything we do, all our deeds and all our works for God, should be a labor of love motivated by our faith and hope in Him.

Good works are meant to be a blessing—not an obligation or a means to salvation. We do good works because of God's love within us, not because we feel pressured to do them. Many people try to work their way to heaven by accomplishing good works. But there is only one way to God, and that is through personal faith in Jesus Christ (John 14:6).

God is not impressed by material gifts or the number of times you help another person. However, He is impressed by the motivation of your heart—that is, love expressing itself through faith.

Good works that hold eternal value are the result of an overflow of your devotion to Christ. If the devotion is there, good works will follow naturally. They never come as a result of self-determination.

When God is evident in your life, the evidence of His good works will be there. Praise, worship, obedience, and prayer are all signs of a heart totally committed to Jesus Christ and overflowing in good works.

Prayer: Dear Lord, let Your presence be evident in my life in my praise, worship, obedience, prayers, and works.

We give thanks to God always for you all, making mention of you in our prayers, remembering without ceasing your work of faith, labor of love, and patience of hope in our Lord Jesus Christ in the sight of our God and Father. (1 Thess. 1:2–3)

Therefore, my beloved brethren, be steadfast, immovable, always abounding in the work of the Lord, knowing that your labor is not in vain in the Lord. (1 Cor. 15:58)

Loving God

The good news of the gospel is not only that God loves us, but that we can love Him too. He told us to love Him like no other. He knew we would serve, obey, and follow the One we love.

Loving God involves affections, that is, the engagement of emotions. Are you stirred in your heart to worship Him as you consider His greatness? Are you occasionally moved to tears by an awareness of His sacrifice for your sin? Is there a sense of awe and wonder deep within as you read His Word and quiet yourself in prayer?

Loving God involves the stimulation of mind. Study, read, and search the Scriptures where He is revealed. You are a disciple, a learner, of who Christ is and what He seeks to do in your life.

Loving God involves the will. You do what He says, whether you feel like it and whether you understand all the implications. The disciples put down their belongings and followed Christ long before they came to full love or knowledge of Him. That is the same lifestyle you are called to imitate today.

God wants you to love Him. He commands you so. You can do this because even when you stumble and fail, He loves you. Knowing that should arouse you to renewed devotion to a Savior who takes great delight in His children.

Prayer: Stir my heart, O God. Let me never lose the sense of wonder and awe of being in Your presence.

Because he has set his love upon Me,
 therefore I will deliver him;
I will set him on high,
 because he has known My name. (Ps. 91:14)

Whom have I in heaven but You?
And there is none upon earth that I desire besides You.
My flesh and my heart fail;
But God is the strength of my heart and my portion forever.
(Ps. 73:25–26)

God's Stabilizing Perspective

The love of God sweeps into your life at salvation, forgiving you of sins and cleansing you from guilt. However, remnants of your old, carnal manner of living cling stubbornly in your inner man.

Most likely, these are long-standing patterns of behavior or emotions that have been entrenched in your mind since childhood. These ingrained practices surface with surprising and irritating regularity.

Before salvation, self-gratification was natural. Once you are saved, self-devotion is still a sticky problem. You find yourself continuing to stake out your turf at the office, demanding your way at home, and centering your activities in a self-pleasing manner.

You need God's stabilizing perspective in this perplexing battle. Once you are born again, all of your problems—particularly habitual, chronic ones—are not automatically eliminated.

The Holy Spirit can strip away the fortifications of sin as you learn to consistently cooperate with His renewing, transforming work. His power, coupled with your patience, can bring great victories.

Prayer: Dear God, strip away the fortifications of sin. Help me cooperate with Your renewing, transforming work in my life.

And now, Israel, what does the LORD your God require of you, but to fear the LORD your God, to walk in all His ways and to love Him, to serve the LORD your God with all your heart and with all your soul. (Deut. 10:12)

For the LORD your God is God of gods and Lord of lords, the great God, mighty and awesome. (Deut. 10:17)

You shall love the LORD your God with all your heart, with all your soul, and with all your strength. (Deut. 6:5)

LOVING FREELY

Although our ability to love is limited, God's capacity for love is endless.

When Jesus sent the twelve disciples out on their first ministry tour, He underscored the significance of sharing the love they had received from the Messiah: "Freely you have received, freely give" (Matt. 10:8).

Perhaps you grew up with uncaring or unaffectionate parents. They loved you but were reluctant to demonstrate their feelings. Quite possibly, their behavior was a reflection of their own parents' orientation. Or maybe you have trouble forgiving those who have treated you unfairly. Maybe you cannot forgive yourself for past behavior, and guilt clogs your emotions.

Your hope for freely extending the love of Jesus is learning to freely receive His love. We are a forgiven people. The Cross washed away all of our sins. You are not under condemnation. Your guilt is vanquished by the soul-cleansing blood of the Lamb, removed forever once you receive Christ as your Savior.

You can freely love, freely serve, freely give, freely forgive, for you are the recipient of such love from the Father. Receive His love, and you cannot keep it from spilling over into the lives of others.

Prayer: Father, thank You for forgiveness and release from condemnation. Thank You for the Cross, which washed away my sin, guilt, and shame.

In all these things we are more than conquerors through Him who loved us. For I am persuaded that neither death nor life, nor angels nor principalities nor powers, nor things present nor things to come, nor height nor depth, nor any other created thing, shall be able to separate us from the love of God which is in Christ Jesus our Lord. (Rom. 8:37–39)

Doctrine Without Love

A school bus backed into a car in a minor neighborhood accident. As the two drivers conversed following the incident, the dialogue turned to a more personal note.

"I used to be a Christian," the bus driver revealed to the inquiring party. "But I was not very wealthy, and most of the people in the church ignored me."

He then explained that he joined another church where the people warmly accepted him but whose doctrine was incompatible with Christianity. Love and false doctrine won over sound doctrine without love. This is a clear danger for evangelicals who often neglect the harmony of the gospel—love—while affirming the lyrics—its teaching.

A Christian's love for the brethren is a major factor in demonstrating the reality of the Christian faith. After all, what is more unnatural (and hence more heavenly) than loving your enemies, admitting when you are wrong, praying for the person who has hurt you, or seeking the welfare of the individual who constantly criticizes you?

Prayer: Father, give me the supernatural ability to love my enemies, admit when I am wrong, pray for those who hurt me, and seek the welfare of those who rise up against me.

All of you be of one mind, having compassion for one another; love as brothers, be tenderhearted, be courteous; not returning evil for evil or reviling for reviling, but on the contrary blessing, knowing that you were called to this, that you may inherit a blessing. For

"He who would love life
And see good days,
Let him refrain his tongue from evil,
And his lips from speaking deceit.
Let him turn away from evil and do good;
Let him seek peace and pursue it." (1 Peter 3:8–11)

Glorifying God

God desires you to be saved for these reasons. The first is that you may know the love of God. God's love is unconditional. Regardless of your circumstances, God loves you. When you refuse His love, you miss the joy of His fellowship and settle for the conditional love of the world.

A second reason God desires you to be saved is to become a trophy of His grace. You are saved by grace through faith. There is nothing you can do to make God love you more than He does at this very moment.

The third reason God wants to save you is that He might be glorified through your life on earth, much as He was through the life of His Son.

The primary purpose for your existence is to bring glory to Christ. When Jesus returns, the Bible says the entire earth will be filled with His glory and the knowledge of Him. You can honor Christ every day as the Holy Spirit works in you as you drive to your job, talk to others over the telephone, and work with those around you.

God is glorified when you share what Jesus did for you on the cross. The only way a lost person knows that God's love is real is by seeing it lived out in the lives of His saints.

Prayer: I want to glorify You, O God. Help me live out in a practical way the manifestation of Your presence in my life.

You are the light of the world. A city that is set on a hill cannot be hidden. Nor do they light a lamp and put it under a basket, but on a lampstand, and it gives light to all who are in the house. Let your light so shine before men, that they may see your good works and glorify your Father in heaven. (Matt. 5:14–16)

A Divine Definition

The thirteenth chapter of Paul's first letter to the Corinthian church is a divine definition of true love. Pleasant words, warm embraces, tearful tugs of the heart, and fun and laughter—while all perfectly legitimate expressions of love—do not necessarily constitute biblical love. True love in God's evaluation exhibits the following characteristics, among others:

Love is patient. Think of God's patience toward you, His long-suffering when you turn aside or stumble. Now, how patient are you toward others? Do you make everyone meet your schedule, or are you willing to work on God's timetable?

Love is kind. God's kindness brought you to repentance and saving faith (Rom. 2:4). Your kindness and good-hearted behavior—regardless of circumstances—can bring others to the Savior as they witness unexpected consideration and thoughtfulness.

The simplicity of God's love is found in your everyday acts of patience and kindness. These are not your virtues but an extension of His Spirit, the godly aroma that makes Christianity attractive and authentic.

Prayer: Lord, please make me patient and kind. Let me demonstrate the simplicity of Your love in everyday acts of kindness.

Do you despise the riches of His goodness, forbearance, and longsuffering, not knowing that the goodness of God leads you to repentance? (Rom. 2:4)

I in them, and You in Me; that they may be made perfect in one, and that the world may know that You have sent Me, and have loved them as You have loved Me. (John 17:23)

Just as you want men to do to you, you also do to them likewise. (Luke 6:31)

UNCONDITIONAL LOVE

Talking and reading about the love of God are inspiring. Practicing God's love, however, is altogether another dimension.

Like a garden, God's love must be cultivated if its fruit is to be genuine, bearing His mark on all of our labors. He supplies the seed, the soil, the nourishment, and He causes the growth. We are only the caretakers.

Oswald Chambers writes in *Our Brilliant Heritage*:

> Neither natural love nor Divine love will remain unless it is cultivated. We must form the habit of love until it is the practice of our lives.
>
> When the Holy Spirit has shed abroad the love of God in our hearts, then that love requires cultivation . . . We have to dedicate ourselves to love, which means identifying ourselves with God's interests in other people.

God's love can be expressed in millions of ways. But its release comes when we gladly deny ourselves and let God be God in us and through us.

God unconditionally loves you, and He wants to unconditionally love others through you. Relax in His love, and make it a habit to give His love away.

Prayer: I want to be dedicated to loving others, Lord. Please shed abroad Your love in my heart through the power of the Holy Spirit.

> If you do good to those who do good to you, what credit is that to you? For even sinners do the same. And if you lend to those from whom you hope to receive back, what credit is that to you? For even sinners lend to sinners to receive as much back. But love your enemies, do good, and lend, hoping for nothing in return; and your reward will be great, and you will be sons of the Most High. For He is kind to the unthankful and evil. (Luke 6:33–35)

Obeying the Father

Just before you leave the house for an overnight trip, your son hugs you and says, "I love you, Dad. Have a good trip."

"I love you, too, Son. Don't forget to clean out the garage like I told you, okay?"

"You bet, Dad."

The next evening you arrive at the door. Your son greets you.

"We missed you, Dad. We love you so much."

"I missed you, too, Son. It's good to see you. Did you get the garage clean as I told you?"

The boy lowers his head.

"No, sir."

Loving God, while definitely a matter of the heart, is gauged ultimately by our obedience to Him. Words of praise and adoration are pleasing to the Father. But the practical test of our love for our heavenly Father comes in whether we do what He asks.

Has God asked you to correct an area of disobedience in your life? Are you participating in an activity that He forbids in His Word? Are you living out the truths of the Scriptures by allowing the Lord Jesus Christ to express His life through you by loving unconditionally, giving generously, serving others, providing godly direction for your children?

Loving God is emotional, but without practical obedience it is incomplete.

Prayer: Father, I want to pass the practical test of love for You. Help me love unconditionally, give generously, and serve others.

> My soul keeps Your testimonies,
> And I love them exceedingly.
> I keep Your precepts and Your testimonies,
> For all my ways are before You. (Ps. 119:167–68)

> The fear of the LORD is the beginning of wisdom;
> A good understanding have all those who do
> His commandments.
> His praise endures forever. (Ps. 111:10)

THE WALK OF LOVE

An old adage rings true of the believer's walk: "People do not care how much you know until they know how much you care."

God's love expressed through the sacrifice of His Son made our salvation possible. His love expressed through the gift of the Holy Spirit makes the abundant life possible.

When the love of God controls you, your love for Him, and His love for you, you are the most settled in your Christian walk and the most effective in your witness.

The walk of love releases others from your expectations. You unconditionally set yourself to exhibit Christ's love regardless of their actions.

The walk of love is expressed in a servant spirit. You look to channel your talents and energies into encouraging and stimulating others. That is unnatural to your fleshly nature and happens only as you are constantly awed by God's love for you.

The walk of love is sacrificial. You are willing to give up your time and even ambition for the sake of seeking first the kingdom of God. You love God first and foremost and thus will prioritize His will and plans.

Walk in love, and your light cannot fail to shine.

Prayer: Dear Father, thank You for Your love expressed through the sacrifice of Your Son and the gift of the Holy Spirit. Thank You for abundant life.

Be imitators of God as dear children. And walk in love, as Christ also has loved us and given Himself for us, an offering and a sacrifice to God for a sweet-smelling aroma. (Eph. 5:1–2)

You, brethren, have been called to liberty; only do not use liberty as an opportunity for the flesh, but through love serve one another. (Gal. 5:13)

A Channel of Love

The grace of God, which has the power to bring a man from the dominion of Satan to the dominion of God, has much potential for exploitation. Used improperly, grace's freedom and forgiveness from sin can be abused.

That was Paul's warning in his letter to the Romans: "What shall we say then? Shall we continue in sin that grace may abound? Certainly not!" (Rom. 6:1–2).

Grace is abused when believers think they can practice sin after salvation. "After all," their argument goes, "I just ask for forgiveness after I sin, and everything is okay." Such reasoning perverts grace and fails to understand that the consequences of sin are still reaped, even by Christians.

Grace is also abused when we fail to extend the same unconditional love to others that God has shown to us. We have been freely forgiven and loved, regardless of our performance. Grace is stunted and derailed in such instances.

A steward of God's grace sees to it that he is a channel of unconditional love to others. The wonder of that grace motivates him to increasing holiness—not sinful indulgence—realizing that grace flows red from the veins of Immanuel.

Prayer: O God, I praise You for Your gift of grace. Let me be a good steward of Your grace.

As each one has received a gift, minister it to one another, as good stewards of the manifold grace of God. (1 Peter 4:10)

What shall we say then? Shall we continue in sin that grace may abound? Certainly not! How shall we who died to sin live any longer in it? (Rom. 6:1–2)

What then? Shall we sin because we are not under law but under grace? Certainly not! (Rom. 6:15)

A Supernatural Love

Christ is our life not only when we are consumed with His agenda but also when His indwelling Spirit reigns within us. Every day, every circumstance, every challenge, every encounter is an opportunity for the believer either to experience the life of Christ or to express his own will, emotions, and opinions apart from the Holy Spirit's wisdom or influence.

The Father and the Son sent the Holy Spirit to bring glory to God by accurately reflecting the ways and character of God. The degree to which we yield to His control is the extent to which we experience Christ as our life. When Christ is our life, the Holy Spirit works through our individual bents and personalities to bring about God's purpose and conform us to His image.

For example, on your job you overhear a friend speaking critically of your work. You are wounded and offended. Later in the day you encounter this person in the break room. You are alone. Anger heaves within, but understanding that forgiveness is the only biblical response, you politely engage in conversation. Perhaps you even pray for that person concerning a special, pressing need. At that very point of obedience—as you yield to the Spirit's direction—you experience the supernatural love of Christ.

Prayer: O Lord, let me be consumed with Your agenda. Let Your Spirit reign within me.

Let the word of Christ dwell in you richly in all wisdom, teaching and admonishing one another in psalms and hymns and spiritual songs, singing with grace in your hearts to the Lord. And whatever you do in word or deed, do all in the name of the Lord Jesus, giving thanks to God the Father through Him. (Col. 3:16–17)

Do not be drunk with wine, in which is dissipation; but be filled with the Spirit. (Eph. 5:18)

A Proper Motive

In the beginning of Jesus' ministry, many people surrounded the Messiah as He preached and ministered. As His date with the cross neared, however, only a few remained by His side.

Those who had initially thronged to His presence eventually returned to their everyday routines because they had sought Him for selfish motives—for healed bodies and full stomachs—hoping Jesus would become "a shining knight" to deliver them from Rome.

Jesus did heal bodies, but the real healing was effected as He was torn on the cross. Jesus did feed the hungry, but His ultimate purpose was to satisfy our spiritual hunger and thirst. Jesus did come to deliver, but from Satan's grip, not Caesar's.

If you are following Christ today only for His blessings or for His power or His provisions, you will eventually be disillusioned. There will come a time when there will be no visible sign of blessing, when every single comfort will be removed. If you have followed Christ for any reason other than loving, loyal obedience, you will be sorely disappointed.

You follow Christ for one foundational reason: He is Lord and King of all, and your allegiance is due Him. That is all that will sustain you when the fish and loaves have ceased.

Prayer: You are Lord and King of all! I give You my allegiance, Lord.

Though He slay me, yet will I trust Him.
Even so, I will defend my own ways before Him. (Job 13:15)

God is our refuge and strength,
A very present help in trouble.
Therefore we will not fear,
Even though the earth be removed,
And though the mountains be
carried into the midst of the sea. (Ps. 46:1–2)

Your Spiritual Inheritance

Many of our homes are filled with precious treasures that were passed down to us from previous generations. Because we have families, we share their legacy in the values and the wisdom they have tried to teach us and even in the material goods they have left behind.

The same concept of a rich spiritual inheritance is repeated throughout Scripture. The singular, wonderful thought expressed is this: all that belongs to Jesus Christ belongs to His saints.

As in most earthly inheritances, two stipulations apply: a death must take place, and we must be family members. Our spiritual inheritance was initiated and made possible by the sacrificial, substitutionary death of Jesus Christ: "He is the Mediator of the new covenant, by means of death . . . that those who are called may receive the promise of the eternal inheritance" (Heb. 9:15).

That inheritance can be enjoyed only by God's children who have placed their faith in Jesus' death and resurrection and thereby have become saints. The believer's inheritance includes the unconditional love of God, forgiveness of his sins, the presence of God in this world, and the riches of eternal life in the age to come. Can any earthly inheritance compare?

Prayer: Heavenly Father, thank You for the tremendous spiritual inheritance I have through Jesus Christ.

Giving thanks to the Father who has qualified us to be partakers of the inheritance of the saints in the light. He has delivered us from the power of darkness and conveyed us into the kingdom of the Son of His love, in whom we have redemption through His blood, the forgiveness of sins. (Col. 1:12–14)

What You Believe

Barricades are ahead. A state trooper stands with his hand and arm outstretched as your car approaches. He leans over and informs you that a bridge has washed out a few miles ahead. You respond, "Look, buddy, I don't believe a word you say. You may look like a state trooper—with the uniform, blue lights, and all—but I don't think you are one, and I'm not going to listen. Please move aside. I've got business to attend to."

What we believe about a person obviously influences our behavior. Similarly what we believe about Jesus Christ determines our behavior on earth as well as our eternal destiny. It is a decision with colossal consequences.

Make no mistake, the primary reason the Pharisees and other Jews didn't bow before the Messiah was that they didn't believe His deity. "We know who You are," they said. "You are the son of Joseph and Mary from Galilee. We also know Your brothers and sisters. You might be a prophet, but the Son of God You certainly are not."

What do you believe about Jesus? Do you think He was a great teacher? A great moral influence? A historic religious leader? Nothing less than accepting and confessing His deity can lead you into the eternal experience of salvation.

Prayer: O God, I confess the deity of Your Son. I believe Jesus Christ is the Savior of the world.

All bore witness to Him, and marveled at the gracious words which proceeded out of His mouth. And they said, "Is this not Joseph's son?" He said to them, "You will surely say this proverb to Me, 'Physician, heal yourself! Whatever we have heard done in Capernaum, do also here in Your country.'" Then He said, "Assuredly, I say to you, no prophet is accepted in his own country." (Luke 4:22–24)

FORGIVING OTHERS

A city police officer was severely wounded in the line of duty. After months of rehabilitation, he was still in a wheelchair where he would very likely spend the rest of his life.

A reporter from a local television station interviewed the officer during a fund-raising drive to help cover his high medical expenses. The reporter asked, "Are you bitter about what has happened to you?" His response was firm: "I do not have any time to waste on feeling bitter."

A bitter spirit does not profit its host; it destroys him. A man who refuses to forgive another has created the ideal climate for the growth of bitterness.

A bitter person can harbor a grudge against his offender for years, a decade, a lifetime, and gain nothing but anger and frustration. Attempts at retaliation only tighten the grip of bitterness.

Forgiveness is the only antidote for a bitter heart. Healing and restoration begin when we release from our judgment the ones who hurt us.

Are you bitter toward someone? Have you been unable to forgive? Today, by God's enabling, forgive the offender, remove the emotional parasite of bitterness from your heart, and release the love of God to flow through you.

Prayer: Dear Lord, remove bitterness and an inability to forgive from my life. Release Your love to flow through me.

Therefore, as the elect of God, holy and beloved, put on tender mercies, kindness, humility, meekness, longsuffering; bearing with one another, and forgiving one another, if anyone has a complaint against another; even as Christ forgave you, so you also must do. But above all these things put on love, which is the bond of perfection. (Col. 3:12–14)

AN AGENT OF LOVE

Officials closed a financial planning corporation after investors reported losing enormous sums. One retired investor lost his life savings—$200,000. Both he and his wife were forced into the workforce to cover their living expenses. In an interview he remarked that his anger had not subsided, and he would remain mad "until the day I die."

His bitterness will affect not only him but also those touched by his life. The venom of bitterness is contagious. A bitter man can infect his family; a bitter employee can communicate hostility to his fellow workers.

That is what makes forgiveness so essential, regardless of the nature of the offense. However cruel and unwarranted your pain may be, forgiveness based on Christ's unconditional love is the most effective healing agent. For the sake of Christ, your sake, and the sake of loved ones, choose by an act of your will to allow the Lord to forgive through you those who have mistreated either you or a loved one.

Christ won your forgiveness by dying on a cross. You forgive by dying to self and becoming an agent for agape love.

Prayer: Dear Lord, help me deny myself and my sinful emotions and become an agent of Your agape love and forgiveness.

Peter came to Him and said, "Lord, how often shall my brother sin against me, and I forgive him? Up to seven times?" Jesus said to him, "I do not say to you, up to seven times, but up to seventy times seven." (Matt. 18:21–22)

Pursue peace with all people, and holiness, without which no one will see the Lord: looking carefully lest anyone fall short of the grace of God; lest any root of bitterness springing up cause trouble, and by this many become defiled. (Heb. 12:14–15)

The Gift of Love

Have you ever tried to help someone who refused your offers? He needed financial assistance but would not accept your gift. He needed a friend but resisted your invitations for fellowship. He needed counsel but rejected your advice.

God's fathomless love is poured out at Calvary's cross. Its life-giving flow is available to everyone. Yet so many refuse the gift of eternal life, turning aside to personal pursuits and pleasures.

Some are deceived. They do not know the truth of the gospel that can set them free. The majority, however, do not respond to God's offer of love because they refuse to admit their need of Him: "I don't need God. I can get along fine without God's help." This reasoning fails to see that apart from personal trust in Christ, man will be judged for his sins and separated from God's presence forever.

Self-sufficiency blinds us to our desperate condition. It taints and spurns the love of God. But God's love still reaches out. The promise of forgiveness, a new birth, and a new relationship with Christ are given instantly when we respond to His love through faith in the sin-bearing Christ.

God loves you. He took the initiative at the cross. Have you received His gift of eternal life?

Prayer: Thank You for Your gift of love, God. Thank You for taking the initiative to extend Your love to me through the Cross.

You shall know the truth, and the truth shall make you free . . . Therefore if the Son makes you free, you shall be free indeed. (John 8:32, 36)

Stand fast therefore in the liberty by which Christ has made us free, and do not be entangled again with a yoke of bondage. (Gal. 5:1)

The Test of Love

Love is a word that has many vague definitions. When we love someone, that can mean we have a certain euphoric feeling. It also can mean we are physically or emotionally attracted to another person.

The Christian who loves God, however, is engaged in far more than mere feelings or emotions. Loving God means obeying His Word and His Spirit: "If anyone loves Me, he will keep My word" (John 14:23).

The acid test of your love for Christ is your obedience to His revealed will. You may say you love God, but do you obey His truth? Your love for God is practically expressed when you obey Him without questioning.

We may not understand God's reasoning, but we are confident in His wisdom. As author Elisabeth Elliot said, "God has not told us everything, but He has told us all we need to know." Such obedience declares our sincere trust in God.

This love is expressed when we obey the Lord despite reasonable alternatives. It is easy to justify and rationalize disobedience when competing paths seem right but are not sanctioned by God. This obedience is a statement of our loyalty to Christ Jesus as Lord.

Is there an area in your life that is not aligned with God's will? If you love God, turn to Him and choose His path.

Prayer: Father, make me obedient to Your Word. Align my life with Your will.

Jesus answered and said to him, "If anyone loves Me, he will keep My word; and My Father will love him, and We will come to him and make Our home with him." (John 14:23)

Teach me, O LORD, the way of Your statutes,
And I shall keep it to the end. (Ps. 119:33)

Teach me Your way, O LORD,
And lead me in a smooth path, because of my enemies.
(Ps. 27:11)

Boasting in God

The more self-reliant we become, the less we seem to acknowledge the goodness of God. Our money pays for our houses and our cars and our children's education. Our skills brought us to this step on the job ladder. If we were thoughtful, we would realize how foolish such reasoning really is.

What did we do to accomplish our existence? Where does the food come from that we put on our tables each day? How did our might create the sun, rain, and mineral-rich soil by which we are nourished?

What expert input did we have in the design of our bodies? Did we weave our hearts, limbs, brains, and organs? What power do we exercise to keep us out of harm's way—to keep away from that drunk driver's car or thief's bullet?

How can we boast in light of such obvious gifts from God? We have done nothing to earn them; we had no part in their creation.

Our skills, income, education, homes—everything—are possible because God acted in love. Yes, we are stewards of His gifts; but the raw material is totally His provision.

Such awareness of God's abundant, unstinting supply should humble you and give birth to your unending gratitude. All you have comes from the hand and heart of a generous and benevolent God. Your boast should be in Him.

Prayer: All I have is from You, Lord. Thank You for Your precious gifts.

You shall remember the LORD your God, for it is He who gives you power to get wealth, that He may establish His covenant which He swore to your fathers, as it is this day. (Deut. 8:18)

Every good gift and every perfect gift is from above, and comes down from the Father of lights, with whom there is no variation or shadow of turning. (James 1:17)

For of Him and through Him and to Him are all things, to whom be glory forever. Amen. (Rom. 11:36)

Objects of God's Love

Jesus' cry of pardon for those who nailed Him to a cross to suffer an agonizing death rings through the centuries: "Father, forgive them, for they do not know what they do" (Luke 23:34). In our humanity we wonder how even the divine Christ could think of such forgiveness for the scornful lot of Pharisees, soldiers, and those who jeered on the hill of Golgotha. Yet we, as disciples of Christ, are called by the Scriptures to be like our Teacher.

Is there anything more difficult? Perhaps not. But are our circumstances any worse than the darkness of Calvary? If forgiveness can be extended in the blackness of the Cross, we can offer it in our shadows of hurt by following Christ's example. Jesus forgave because He knew sin's deceit was at work in His persecutors. When people offend us, they do not fully understand the folly of their ways, the deceitfulness of sin, and the consequences of their actions.

Christ forgave because He had come to die for the sins of all men, including those who nailed Him to a tree. You forgive because you are called to love all men—even your enemies—knowing they, too, are objects of God's seeking love. You can forgive because the forgiving Christ is within you.

Prayer: Lord, I thank You for the forgiving Christ, who dwells within me and gives me the ability to offer the gifts of love and forgiveness to others.

Then Jesus said, "Father, forgive them, for they do not know what they do." And they divided His garments and cast lots. (Luke 23:34)

Whenever you stand praying, if you have anything against anyone, forgive him, that your Father in heaven may also forgive you your trespasses. But if you do not forgive, neither will your Father in heaven forgive your trespasses. (Mark 11:25–26)

RELATING TO OTHERS

In her booklet entitled *Relationships*, Pamela Reeve writes:

> Not long ago I walked by a wall poster that brought me back for a second look. I can't remember the artwork, but I've never forgotten the pithy, pointed message: "Involvement with people is always a very delicate thing . . . It requires real maturity to become involved and not get all messed up."
>
> How true! And yet there is nothing more important than involvement with other people. In fact, you can't be rightly related to God without being rightly related to other people. The very test of my relationship with God is my relationship with other people.

If we want to know how to relate to others in a loving and caring way, we must first come to understand and identify with the Father's love. He was not afraid of getting "messed up" with us. Throughout the New Testament, we see how Jesus moved among the people. No sin was too great for His forgiveness; no affliction too grave for His healing touch. He is the Master Friend who laid His life down for you. This is God's loving intent, that you would know and share this same love with others.

Oswald Chambers wrote, "It is impossible to weary God's love, and it is impossible to weary that love in me if it springs from the one center." Let your love spring from God so that others will see His goodness.

Prayer: O Lord, let me pass the test of my relationship with You by properly relating to others.

The Spirit of the LORD is upon Me,
Because He has anointed Me
To preach the gospel to the poor;
He has sent Me to heal the brokenhearted,
To proclaim liberty to the captives
And recovery of sight to the blind,
To set at liberty those who are oppressed. (Luke 4:18)

Now it happened, as Jesus sat at the table in the house, that behold, many tax collectors and sinners came and sat down with Him and His disciples. (Matt. 9:10)

When Jesus heard that, He said to them, "Those who are well have no need of a physician, but those who are sick. But go and learn what this means: 'I desire mercy and not sacrifice.' For I did not come to call the righteous, but sinners, to repentance." (Matt. 9:12–13)

FRIENDSHIP WITH GOD

The older man and the young boy were good friends. They often worked together in the man's crowded woodworking shop, piecing together intricate designs for local craft shops.

One day the boy stole several wood chisels from the shop. Looking through his kitchen window, the man witnessed the incident but said nothing about it. Thereafter, the man and the boy met together infrequently. When they did, the boy was distant and hesitant. Their friendship was broken.

When we sin against God, the most ominous consequence is not the act itself but the damage done to our intimate relationship with Him. God saved us so that we might once again fellowship with Him. The precious fatherhood of God and our friendship with God are two of salvation's best results.

If you have sinned against God, do not hesitate to come quickly to Him and ask His forgiveness. His love knows no limits. Failure to humble yourself inevitably leads to a cooling of your intimacy with God.

God is waiting for you to return. His loving-kindness is everlasting; His mercies are fresh and new each morning. Restore your intimacy and your relationship with your best possible Friend.

Prayer: I want to be Your friend, Father. Thank You for Your loving-kindness and Your mercies, which are renewed to me each morning.

If we say that we have no sin, we deceive ourselves, and the truth is not in us. If we confess our sins, He is faithful and just to forgive us our sins and to cleanse us from all unrighteousness. If we say that we have not sinned, we make Him a liar, and His word is not in us. (1 John 1:8–10)

Loving Freely

In his book *Inside Out,* Dr. Larry Crabb describes some of the results of not opening up to the Lord and others in genuine love:

> A person's style of relating [to others] is like the proverbial snowflake—no two are exactly alike. The design reflected in all of them is the underlying motivation of either self-protection or love . . . If the core business of life is to love each other as God loves us, then a priority effort to play it safe interferes with the purpose of living.
>
> We were designed to love and when we do, something good develops inside. We feel clean, rich, whole. Even better, we become less concerned with how we feel and more concerned with the lives of others. But when a commitment to self-protection governs what we say, how we say it, and to whom, then a nagging discomfort creeps through our soul that demands to be soothed . . . We were designed by a God who wants us to trust His love enough to freely love others, not to protect our longings from further injury.

What if the Samaritan woman at the well had decided not to talk to Jesus? She had much to hide, but Jesus' words were so tantalizing to her lonely soul that she asked Him where to find the living water. By opening up in conversation, she allowed Him to impact her life. Had she chosen to protect herself, she would have missed the Messiah.

Prayer: Father, I open my heart and spirit to You today. I don't want to miss Your divine visitation.

> For the Son of Man has come to seek and to save that which was lost. (Luke 19:10)

> Then the woman of Samaria said to Him, "How is it that You, being a Jew, ask a drink from me, a Samaritan woman?" For Jews have no dealings with Samaritans. Jesus answered and said to her, "If you knew the gift of God, and who it is who says to you, 'Give Me a drink,' you would have asked Him, and He would have given you living water." (John 4:9–10)

He Comes to Us

One of the first people to whom Jesus revealed Himself as the Messiah was the Samaritan woman. Usually, Jews looked down on the Samaritans because they were a mixed race—part Jew and part Greek. They also refused to worship at the temple in Jerusalem. However, this woman was of special interest to Jesus. She had been married five times, and the man she was with at that point was not her husband. Warren Wiersbe writes,

> Because He was on a divinely appointed schedule, it was necessary that Jesus go through Samaria. Why? Because He would meet a woman there and lead her into saving faith, the kind of true faith that would affect an entire village. Our Lord was no respecter of persons. Earlier, He counseled a moral Jewish man (John 3), and now He would witness to an immoral Samaritan woman! . . . In that day, it was not considered proper for any man, especially a rabbi, to speak in public to a strange woman. But our Lord set social customs aside because a soul's eternal salvation was at stake.

Jesus had only one purpose in mind when He came to earth, and that was to rescue us from sin. Through the life of this woman, we are given a picture of ourselves. Each of us deserves death, but because of God's mercy and grace, He has granted us life. Each of us is the woman at the well, and just as He came to her, He comes to each of us.

Prayer: Lord, thank You for coming to me. Thank You for Your gifts of mercy, grace, and abundant life.

> Therefore, just as through one man sin entered the world, and death through sin, and thus death spread to all men, because all sinned. (Rom. 5:12)

> Yes, we had the sentence of death in ourselves, that we should not trust in ourselves but in God who raises the dead, who delivered us from so great a death, and does deliver us; in whom we trust that He will still deliver us. (2 Cor. 1:9–10)

Proclaiming the Message of Salvation

The apostle Paul had a passion to proclaim Jesus Christ as the Messiah. God instructed him to take the gospel to the Gentiles, which he did, but he also wanted the Jews to know the Messiah had come. Therefore, as he entered each city, the first place Paul stopped was the local synagogue. Even though some of the Jews were attracted to his message, most refused God's message of salvation. They went on to attack and harm Paul for preaching what they believed was heresy in light of the law that God gave to Moses.

At Lystra (Acts 14:8–19) they sought to stone Paul to death! But God strengthened His servant. Instead of becoming discouraged, he became more convinced that what he was doing was right in line with God's will.

If you are facing extreme opposition because of your commitment to the Lord Jesus Christ, then take courage. God will never leave you to face any situation alone. His goal in adversity is to teach you to keep your eyes on Him regardless of what others around you are doing. Paul lived so that Christ could be proclaimed through him. And Paul was willing to risk death to get the message out.

Each Christian is called to proclaim the message of salvation. Have you settled this issue within your heart? Are you allowing Christ to flow through you so that others can see His life-changing love?

Prayer: Dear heavenly Father, let the Spirit of Your Son flow through me so that others can see the manifestation of His life-changing love.

The Lord stood with me and strengthened me, so that the message might be preached fully through me, and that all the Gentiles might hear. And I was delivered out of the mouth of the lion. (2 Tim. 4:17)

We do not want you to be ignorant, brethren, of our trouble which came to us in Asia: that we were burdened beyond measure, above strength, so that we despaired even of life. (2 Cor. 1:8)

The Holy Spirit testifies in every city, saying that chains and tribulations await me. (Acts 20:23)

Reflecting His Love

Our passion to proclaim Jesus Christ must be able to withstand the test of time if we are to complete the work He has called us to do. You may be a mother whose day rolls by at a frantic pace. God has given you a tremendous opportunity to be a godly influence in the lives of your family members.

Only a true passion to proclaim Him can survive piles of dirty dishes and clothes and the endless drives to drop children off at school and band practice. It is the passion to know and love Jesus Christ that others see even in the smallest of things. Children love to imitate their parents. What they see in your life is more important than a thousand textbooks.

No matter who we are or what occupation we have, the passion to tell others about the hope we have needs to be at the forefront of all we do and say. You may be a top executive who refuses to give in to mounting pressure to compromise your Christian convictions. Don't lose sight of the fact that your life is a testimony to someone else.

You don't always have to preach with words to make Christ known. God uses the entirety of your life as a reflection of His personal love for you. Therefore, keep your eyes on Jesus. Find encouragement in His presence, and He will proclaim His message through you.

Prayer: Help me keep my eyes on You, Lord. Encourage me, then let me proclaim Your message to a hurting world.

You are our epistle written in our hearts, known and read by all men; clearly you are an epistle of Christ, ministered by us, written not with ink but by the Spirit of the living God, not on tablets of stone but on tablets of flesh, that is, of the heart. And we have such trust through Christ toward God. Not that we are sufficient of ourselves to think of anything as being from ourselves, but our sufficiency is from God. (2 Cor. 3:2–5)

GIVING YOURSELF AWAY

What is your motivation for being generous? Is it to serve God and others, or is it to fulfill a need within yourself? If it is to serve God, you will find that sincere giving requires letting go of personal expectations.

When you give materially, give with a cheerful heart. When you give emotionally, don't place expectations on others. Let your giving be free and unattached to do's and don'ts. Allow God to be sovereign in the lives of those you touch each day. The benchmark of generosity is a godly desire to bless someone else.

A truly generous person doesn't look for a thank-you note in the mail. They are not waiting by the telephone for personal praise. Although it is nice to know that God has used you, it is even more rewarding to know you have given of yourself in such a way that another has felt the love and grace of Christ.

God wants you to be a giver. He gave His greatest gift to you through the life, death, and resurrection of His Son. Jesus lives within you through the power of the Holy Spirit, and He will teach you how to give yourself away.

You may think, *I have nothing to offer,* but you do. You can give yourself to a friend, a coworker, a neighbor, or maybe someone you really don't know that well. Take time to listen to those who are facing disappointment. Ask God to help you, and He will show you who needs His touch of love today.

Prayer: Lord, I am so insensitive to others at times. Teach me to give the way You gave of Yourself.

There is one who scatters, yet increases more;
And there is one who withholds more than is right,
But it leads to poverty.
The generous soul will be made rich,
And he who waters will also be watered himself.
(Prov. 11:24–25)

Give, and it will be given to you: good measure, pressed down, shaken together, and running over will be put into your bosom. For with the same measure that you use, it will be measured back to you. (Luke 6:38)

Loving Others

God is not afraid to love us just the way we are, with all our flaws and shortcomings. He is secure in who He is. Therefore, He loves us unconditionally and without regard to our failures.

He created us not to live apart from His love but to be partakers of His holiness. However, He knows that there will be times when we look and act very unholy. Our misguided actions do not erase or stop the love of God. Sin can separate us from His blessings and intimate fellowship, but there is never a time when God withholds His love.

In loving us, God knows that we can never give back to Him what He has given to us, but He requires us to love one another with the same love that He has demonstrated toward us.

In his book *Mighty Is Your Hand*, David Hazard paraphrases the words of Andrew Murray:

> In our life with people, the one thing on which everything depends is love. The spirit of forgiveness is the spirit of love. Because God is love, He forgives. Consequently, it is only as we are dwelling in the love of God that we can forgive as God forgives.
>
> Our love for others is the evidence of our love for God. It is our grounds for confidence before God in prayer. It our assurance that our prayer will be heard (1 John 4:15). Let the

love you have for God be a symbol of love and forgiveness to all you meet.

Prayer: Dear Lord, let my love for You be a symbol of Your divine love and forgiveness to everyone I meet today.

If someone says, "I love God," and hates his brother, he is a liar; for he who does not love his brother whom he has seen, how can he love God whom he has not seen? And this commandment we have from Him: that he who loves God must love his brother also. (1 John 4:20–21)

By this we know that we love the children of God, when we love God and keep His commandments. (1 John 5:2)

ELIMINATING LOVE'S ENEMIES

Two of the greatest enemies of love are jealousy and the need to have things our own way. In 1 Corinthians 13:11, Paul compared attitudes like these to those of a child, and in doing so he told his audience to "put away childish things."

In *The Sensation of Being Somebody*, Maurice Wagner writes,

> The most common problem in relationships seems to be the trait of attempting to control those we love. When a person does this, he becomes possessive, jealous, and often demanding. This is commonly understood to be a mark of immaturity, and it is.
>
> If we are to overcome this tendency to resent loss of control, we must deal with the resentment. We do not accomplish this by blaming ourselves for being too controlling. We need to let go of the infantile rage of always having to have our own way, identify it by seeing it for what it is, and dissipate it by determining a more productive way of coping.
>
> After we do this, we can reaffirm our faith in God's control of everything that happens to us, and try to accept what happens as being our responsibility under God to hold steady and try to resolve our frustrations without so much anger . . . We can lay aside our anger, wrath, and malice more easily when we return to our securities in Christ.

Prayer: Father, cleanse me of jealousy and selfishness. Help me put away these childish attitudes.

When I was a child, I spoke as a child, I understood as a child, I thought as a child; but when I became a man, I put away childish things. (1 Cor. 13:11)

Be kindly affectionate to one another with brotherly love, in honor giving preference to one another. (Rom. 12:10)

For jealousy is a husband's fury;
Therefore he will not spare in the day of vengeance.
(Prov. 6:34)

Connecting to His Love

The house was in the pathway of the storm. As the winds swept through the trees, the telephone and electrical lines were blown and stretched to the point of separation. Finally the few lines connected to the electrical transformer gave way, and darkness covered what was once light.

God created us to live in the light of His love. He never meant for the storms of life to alienate us from Him. Many unbelievers have yet to experience His warmth and care because past sins, too dark to mention, separate them from Love's true power. Only Jesus has the ability to erase the sins of your past and offer you a fresh, new start at life.

Stop counting the injustices done against you and the sins you have committed. The past belongs to God; there is nothing you can do to change it. But you can ask Him to forgive you and allow His cleansing power to breathe fresh, new hope and forgiveness into your life.

There is nothing stronger than God's love—not sin, certainly not the enemy, or any part of your past. Ask God to teach you how to forgive yourself and then how to enjoy His love. His love will set you free from feelings of guilt and shame. This is the power of love that no storm can quench. When you are connected to the love of Christ, you are eternally on-line to the heart of God.

Prayer: Father, show me how to forgive myself and enjoy Your love. Set me free from guilt and shame.

Whoever hears these sayings of Mine, and does them, I will liken him to a wise man who built his house on the rock: and the rain descended, the floods came, and the winds blew and beat on that house; and it did not fall, for it was founded on the rock. But everyone who hears these sayings of Mine, and does not do them, will be like a foolish man who built his house on the sand: and the rain descended, the floods came, and the winds blew and beat on that house; and it fell. And great was its fall. (Matt. 7:24–27)

Restoring Broken Intimacy

It happened in the spring of the year, at the time when kings go out to battle (2 Sam. 11:1). Sounds like the beginning of a short story, doesn't it? One can imagine the springtime when flowers bud and days are warm and docile. But these words are anything but fragrant. They represent the prelude to broken intimacy.

David stayed in Jerusalem while other kings were out doing kingly things. An evening stroll across the palace roof revealed a young woman bathing in a small pool. David stood where many stand today. The temptation was so great that for a moment's pleasure, he risked damaging his intimate relationship with God.

Broken intimacy—how do we deal with it? The best way is preventive maintenance. Peter was serious when he wrote: "Be sober, be vigilant; because your adversary the devil walks about like a roaring lion, seeking whom he may devour. Resist him, steadfast in the faith" (1 Peter 5:8–9).

All sin begins in the mind. The best way to ward off temptation is to catch it the moment it begs entry to your thoughts (2 Cor. 10:5). Ask God to give you the strength to say no. If you do fall, confess your sin to Christ. Ask Him to restore your fellowship by the power of His grace. David's heart was grieved by his actions, but God in His mercy brought restoration and hope.

Prayer: Dear Lord, help me remain alert to the adversary. Strengthen my faith, so I can effectively resist his attacks.

Casting down arguments and every high thing that exalts itself against the knowledge of God, bringing every thought into captivity to the obedience of Christ. (2 Cor. 10:5)

Be sober, be vigilant; because your adversary the devil walks about like a roaring lion, seeking whom he may devour. Resist him, steadfast in the faith, knowing that the same sufferings are experienced by your brotherhood in the world. (1 Peter 5:8–9)

FOSTERING CHRISTIAN RELATIONSHIPS

The woman told her pastor of a struggle she was having with a longtime Christian friend. For years the friend had battled feelings of depression. The situation often appeared hopeless. Though she tried to encourage her friend, nothing seemed to work for any length of time. Thoughts of ending the friendship filled the woman's mind, but she lacked the peace to do so.

Once, while shopping for a card for her friend's birthday, the woman cried out to God, "All the cards are filled with words of joy and encouragement. How can I give her one of these when she refuses to believe a single word I say? Lord, You will have to show me the kind of card You want me to give."

Suddenly this thought came to her: *Give her a card like you would want Me to give you.* Most of us love to have friends who make us feel good about ourselves. People who have money, time, and energy usually know how to draw a crowd. But the hidden truth here is that very few, if any of us, live a life untouched by heartache and pain.

Charles Spurgeon, Amy Carmichael, A. B. Simpson, Corrie ten Boom, and even Catherine Marshall fought feelings of despair. Beside each person was a friend willing to weather stormy times with him. Christian relationships are not fluffy; they are true to the nature of Christ—willing to bear pain and grief as easily as share joy and blessing.

Prayer: Lord, help me be a good friend, even in difficult times. Show me the value of Christian relationships.

If one member suffers, all the members suffer with it; or if one member is honored, all the members rejoice with it. (1 Cor. 12:26)

Choosing rather to suffer affliction with the people of God than to enjoy the passing pleasures of sin. (Heb. 11:25)

Yet if anyone suffers as a Christian, let him not be ashamed, but let him glorify God in this matter. (1 Peter 4:16)

ELIMINATING BARRIERS

Robert Frost, in his poem "Mending Wall," talks about the subtle problems that occur when barriers are erected in relationships:

Something there is that doesn't love a wall . . .
My apple trees will never get across
And eat the cones under his pines, I tell him.
He only says, "Good fences make good neighbors."

Piling one stone on top of another to make a strong wall, this man was trying in his own way to ensure that he would not be taken advantage of by his neighbor next door. But in the process of protecting himself from potential harm, he also blocked out the blessing of free and open fellowship.

Have you ever chosen the "safe" method of maintaining relationships? It is easier to keep a polite distance from those around you than it is to risk the possibility of injury, especially if you were hurt by a certain person before.

Jesus has a different plan for friendships, one that includes initiating reconciliation, even when someone else holds a grudge against you. If a friend puts up an emotional wall because of an offense, whether real or perceived, you are responsible for helping tear it down. Only then can you build the kind of relationship based on Jesus' principle of unconditional love.

Can you feel the stones from a wall constructed against you? Ask the Lord for steps to take to pull it down. God is the One who does not love a wall.

Prayer: Father, in the name of Jesus, I tear down every wall that has been constructed against me. Break down the barriers!

> I say to you that whoever is angry with his brother without a cause shall be in danger of the judgment. And whoever says to his brother, "Raca!" shall be in danger of the council. But whoever says, 'You fool!' shall be in danger of hell fire. Therefore if you bring your gift to the altar, and there remember that your brother has something against you, leave your gift there before the altar, and go your way. First be reconciled to your brother, and then come and offer your gift. (Matt. 5:22–24)

YOUR SINGLE GREATEST NEED

What would you list as your single greatest need today? A new house? A better job? A marriage partner? A genuine friend? An increase in income? What if that need were dramatically met before this day was over? You moved into a beautiful home, got the job you wanted, found the perfect mate, met a true friend, and came into a healthy inheritance. Would you still have a pressing need in a week or two?

We're never without needs. That's why the answer to the original question–"What would you list as your single greatest need today?"—can be only an intimate, steadfast, growing relationship with Jesus Christ. That is our greatest need.

When we know Christ, we can have all of our emotional needs met. He said, "Come to Me, all you who labor and are heavy laden, and I will give you rest" (Matt. 11:28).

When we make knowing God our chief priority, our physical needs are met: "But seek first the kingdom of God and His righteousness, and all these things [clothing, food, drink, the necessities of life] shall be added to you" (Matt. 6:33).

To know God is to have a vital relationship with the Author, Sustainer, and End of all things. That is really the only necessary thing. Is it yours?

Prayer: O God, give me a vital relationship with You as the Author, Sustainer, and End of all things. That is my greatest need.

Martha was distracted with much serving, and she approached Him and said, "Lord, do You not care that my sister has left me to serve alone? Therefore tell her to help me." And Jesus answered and said to her, "Martha, Martha, you are worried and troubled about many things. But one thing is needed, and Mary has chosen that good part, which will not be taken away from her." (Luke 10:40–42)

Soldiers of the Lord

Do you have a passion to serve God? He may not call you into the ministry or to the foreign mission field. However, He calls all of us to serve Him daily with our lives. Often this requires much more of us than we are willing to give.

Charles Spurgeon wrote,

> The Lord always trains His soldiers, not by letting them lie on feather-beds, but by turning them out, and using them in forced marches and hard service. He makes them ford through streams, and swim through rivers, and climb mountains, and walk many a long march with heavy knapsacks of sorrow on their backs.
>
> This is the way in which He makes them soldiers—not by dressing them up in fine uniforms, to swagger at the barracks gates, and to be fine gentlemen in the eyes of the loungers in the park. God knows that soldiers are only to be made in battle; they are not to be grown in peaceful times.
>
> We may grow the stuff of which soldiers are made; but warriors are really educated by the smell of powder, in the midst of whizzing bullets, not in soft and peaceful times. Well Christian, may not this account for it all? Is not the Lord bringing out your graces and making them grow: Is He not developing in you the qualities of the soldier by throwing you into the heat of battle, and should you not use every appliance to come off conqueror?

Prayer: Give me my marching orders, Lord. Make me a good soldier in Your spiritual army.

> He gives power to the weak,
> And to those who have no might He increases strength.
> Even the youths shall faint and be weary,
> And the young men shall utterly fall,
> But those who wait on the LORD
> Shall renew their strength;
> They shall mount up with wings like eagles,
> They shall run and not be weary,
> They shall walk and not faint. (Isa. 40:29–31)

The Right Decision

Can you imagine what it was like to sit at the feet of Jesus? Mary of Bethany knew. So did Peter and James and John. They all knew what it was like to abide in the love of God, yet even though Jesus was with them, they did not have the fullness of God living within them through the presence of the Holy Spirit.

We are blessed because the Holy Spirit resides in all who believe in God's Son. You may be thinking: *Yes, but I am so easily drawn away by temptation. I know I love God, but there seem to be so many other things that grab my attention. How can I experience His love personally?*

Mary was at the Savior's feet because she made the right decision. God's love drew her, but she chose to be there. Martha had the same opportunity, but she chose instead to work, trying to please Jesus and win His affection.

When she felt left out, Martha complained, to which Jesus replied, "Martha, Martha, you are worried and troubled about many things. But one thing is needed, and Mary has chosen that good part, which will not be taken away from her" (Luke 10:41–42).

Those who sit at the feet of Jesus choose humble devotion over the performance of great deeds. Love is simple here. There are not long lists to be completed, but only one demand—seek the love of God with all of your heart.

Prayer: Help me make the right choice, Father. Let me continually remain at Your feet and rejoice in Your gift of love.

O God, You are my God;
Early will I seek You;
My soul thirsts for You;
My flesh longs for You
In a dry and thirsty land
Where there is no water. (Ps. 63:1)

Blessed are those who keep His testimonies,
Who seek Him with the whole heart! (Ps. 119:2)

Let all those who seek You rejoice and be glad in You;
And let those who love Your salvation say continually,
"Let God be magnified!" (Ps. 70:4)

About the Author

Dr. Charles Stanley is pastor of the 15,000-member First Baptist Church in Atlanta, Georgia. He is well known through his *In Touch* radio and television ministry to thousands internationally and is the author of many books, including *On Holy Ground, Our Unmet Needs, Into His Presence, Enter His Gates, The Source of My Strength, The Reason for My Hope, How to Listen to God,* and *How to Handle Adversity.*

Dr. Stanley received his bachelor of arts degree from the University of Richmond, his bachelor of divinity degree from Southwestern Theological Seminary, and his master's and doctor's degrees from Luther Rice Seminary. He has twice been elected president of the Southern Baptist Convention.

OLD TESTAMENT SCRIPTURES CITED

NEW TESTAMENT SCRIPTURES CITED

Other Books by Charles Stanley from Thomas Nelson Publishers

Enter His Gates
Eternal Security
The Gift of Forgiveness
The Glorious Journey
How to Handle Adversity
How to Keep Your Kids on Your Team
How to Listen to God

The In Touch Study Series
Advancing Through Adversity
Becoming Emotionally Whole
Developing a Servant's Heart
Developing Inner Strength
Discovering Your Identity in Christ
Experiencing Forgiveness
Experiencing Success God's Way
Exploring the Depths of God's Love
Feeling Secure in a Troubled World
Listening to God
Living in His Sufficiency
Ministering Through Spiritual Gifts
Overcoming the Enemy
Practicing Basic Spiritual Disciplines
Protecting Your Family
Relying on the Holy Spirit
Sharing the Gift of Encouragement
Talking with God
Understanding Eternal Security
Understanding Financial Stewardship
Winning on the Inside

In Touch with God
Into His Presence
Our Unmet Needs
The Power of the Cross
The Reason for My Hope
Success God's Way
The Source of My Strength
Winning the War Within
The Wonderful Spirit-Filled Life

The Power of the Cross

Using inspirational Scriptures as well as personal insights and heartfelt prayers, Charles Stanley encourages you to see the transforming power of the Resurrection for salvation, victory over temptation, healing of emotional pain, and restoration with the heavenly Father.

0-7852-7065-6 • Printed Hardcover • 208 pages • Gift/Devotional

The Reason for My Hope

Dr. Stanley shares his personal struggles to remain focused on Christ and keep hope alive in the middle of difficult circumstances. In his warm and insightful style, he reveals the promises and resources God provides His children, identifying nine key reasons for all believers to have unshakable hope.

0-8407-7765-5 • Hardcover • 256 pages • Christian Living

Into His Presence

Into His Presence is a daily devotional from one of America's most respected pastors. Through these powerful insights Dr. Stanley helps readers move out of the valley and leads them to new heights of intimacy with God.

0-7852-6854-5 • Hardcover • 400 pages • Devotional